Incarnational Spirituality

A strategy to bless our world

The text of this book is from an online class called **Are You Ready to Change Your World?**

Other books by
David Spangler

Blessing: The Art and the Practice

The Call

Parent as Mystic - Mystic as Parent

Manifestation: Creating the life you love

The Story Tree

Starshaman Home Mystery School™ Textbook Series

- *Home-Crafting: Self, Sacred and Blessing*
- *Space-Crafting: The Incarnational Self*
- *Crafting Inner Alliances: Working with Spiritual Forces**
- *World-Crafting: Manifestation and Service**

* In Progress

Incarnational Spirituality

A strategy to bless our world

This Lorian Textbook is the transcript of an online class called *Are You Ready to Change Your World?* It has minimal editing to preserve the flavor of the original class. The content has been shaped in part by the unique nature of the class itself.

David Spangler

Incarnational Spirituality

A strategy to bless our world

Copyright © 2008 David Spangler

All rights reserved, including the right to reproduce this book, or portions thereof, in any form.

Edited by Jeremy Berg

Published by Lorian Press
2204 E Grand Ave.
Everett, WA 98201

ISBN: 0-936878-21-5
978-0-936878-21-8

Spangler/David
Incarnational Spirituality/David Spangler

Printed in the United States of America

0 9 8 7 6 5 4 3 2 1

www.lorian.org

Dedication

This book is dedicated to all those who read this book, practice the exercises and make positive changes to bless themselves and our world.

Contents

Chapter One: Introduction to Incarnational Spirituality ... 1

Exercise One: The Empty Stage 12
Exercise Two: Creating a Boundary 16

Chapter Two: More On Incarnation 20

Exercise Three: Standing 42

Chapter Three: Terms and Definitions 46

Exercise Four: Self-Light 60
Exercise Five: Blessing or "Sourcing" 66
Exercise Six: Alternate "Sourcing" 67

Chapter Four: Holding and Blessing............................... 71

Exercise Seven: The Lap 74
Exercise Eight: The Sphere of Holding and Blessing 78

Chapter Five: The Incarnational Field 82

Exercise Nine: Holding and Blessing
                 Your Incarnational Field 90

Chapter Six: Touching the Earth 96

Exercise Ten: The Holding Touch 100
Exercise Eleven: Massaging the World 103

Chapter Seven: Summation 107

Chapter One
Introduction to Incarnational Spirituality

Incarnational Spirituality is the art and practice of evoking and using inner resources of energy arising from the act of incarnation itself order to shape one's life, bless one's world, and become a partner with the creative forces of spirit. Parts of this approach may seem familiar to you and other parts may seem new. Most of the material that makes up this approach comes out of my intuitive and clairvoyant research sustained over many years of interaction with subtle, supersensory, non-physical beings and realms. Arising from a partnership with spiritual worlds does not give this material any special authority as "revelation," or any special, infallible authenticity. Like the fruits of any research, the insights that make up Incarnational Spirituality need to be tested in an individual's life to determine their usefulness or accuracy for that individual. Without such testing, they remain hypotheses.

The research of Incarnational Spirituality is ongoing and a work-in-progress. I and the faculty and students of Lorian have been testing and living this spirituality for years with positive effects and are confident of its value to add meaning to a person's life and service to the world. Using Incarnational Spirituality as our foundation and philosophy, we have been teaching classes ranging from one-day workshops to our year long programs and have seen the benefits people have received from this approach.

A strategy to bless our World
~ Three Levels of Change ~

Incarnational Spirituality is more than a personal spiritual practice for inner development or private attunement. It is also a way of giving service and of enhancing our capacities to serve. It is a way of bringing change into our world, beginning with ourselves. There are three levels of change that Incarnational Spirituality explores:

1. Inner Change: This is the change we can make in our personal Self. These are changes of worldview, attitude, orientation, and energy. A central element of Incarnational Spirituality is the shift we can make within ourselves that opens us to the generative power and energy of our own incarnational spirit.

2. Individual Life Change: This is the change we can bring to the shape of our lives and to our immediate relationships and environment. Two examples of this are the arts of manifestation and blessing.

3. World Work or Change in the World: Using the resources of our incarnational spirit, we add our energies to the inner and outer forces of change in the world.

Incarnational Spirituality arises from these basic premises:

1. The act of incarnation is the primal act from that creation that emerges from the Generative Mystery of the Sacred. The cosmos is the incarnation of the Sacred.

2. Our individual acts of incarnation are a fractal or resonant expression of this primal sacred act, a means by which we participate in and manifest sacredness ourselves.

3. Incarnation is more than a singular event, i.e., the means by which we become physical individuals through birth into this world. Incarnational Spirituality is a process that is ongoing.

4. The act of incarnation generates creative energy. Consequently, our act of incarnating into this world released a burst of spiritual and vital energy that is part of who we are. It is an inner resource upon which we can draw.

5. At the heart of the incarnational process is a generative source that is the essence of Self, our sacred individuality and sovereignty. This Sovereignty is present and can be tapped within all manifestations of Self, from the mystery and depths of the Soul to the everyday

expressions of the personality.

6. An objective of Incarnational Spirituality is to understand and inhabit all levels of Self with love and honor as a means of unfolding the coherency and power of our unique spiritual Presence as a blessing in the world.

7. Incarnation is an act of resonance between the individual and the universal. Incarnational Spirituality calls us to use our own incarnational process and sovereignty to partner with, participate in, and enhance the universal and sacred spirit of Incarnation itself, in honor, blessing, and empowerment for all the other acts of incarnation that make up our world.

Where do these premises come from?

Here's a personal story. When I first began my public work as a teacher in 1965, I entered into a partnership with a non-physical being whom I called "John." I could see and communicate with this being through the use of senses operating beyond the range of our normal physical senses. I have always been able to do this to some degree my entire life. As a child, I thought the inner worlds were simply a normal part of the world as a whole. John was a friend, partner, and mentor who helped me sharpen and discipline my inner senses so that they became more effective tools in doing the spiritual research and investigation that has been my particular calling in life.

One day early in our relationship, he said to me, "You do not simply receive spiritual energies from God or from transpersonal sources. You are yourself, as an incarnate individual, a source of spiritual energy. Human beings are not simply conduits for spiritual forces from higher levels to pass through you into the world; each person is a unique generative source of such forces in ways appropriate to the world in which you live." I confess this didn't mean much to me at the time, other than as an affirmation of the value and importance of each individual.

Some years later, I became aware, first with the people with whom I was working in classes and then subsequently with people whom I just met in the course of my everyday activities, that there was a subtle energy around them that seemed new to me. It was an inner phenomenon I didn't recognize. It was a spiritual energy that was akin to the kind of energies that came from higher, non-physical levels, but it did not seem to be coming from that realm so as far as I could determine. Investigating this, I discovered that it did not come from a transpersonal aspect of the individual but was emerging from the inner dynamics of the personal life. The incarnate life as individuals engaged with their world was not an emotional or mental energy but a spiritual force capable of empowerment and blessing the same as any spiritual force originating in the higher realms. I called this force the "empersonal spirit," meaning that it was arising from or emerging out of the personal dimension of our lives, rather than, say, the transpersonal. It became a key element in how I taught the art of blessing, as described in my book of that name.

As I continued to explore and work with this energy, my perceptions went deeper. I realized that this energy initially emerged from the act of incarnating into the physical realm. It was as if we crossed a boundary when coming into this world and in doing so triggered a release of energy from the spirit of the world itself that then became part of our own individual pattern. I discovered that this empersonal spirit was not the whole picture.

In investigating this empersonal spirit, I recalled something John had said some years before. I found myself touching a generative source of Light and spiritual energy within the life of each person. This source was not quite the same thing as the "sacred within" or the soul or a "higher self," though as a spiritual energy it had obvious connections and resonance with all of these. What it seemed to be was the quality of "source-ness" or of being a generative source itself. It was intimately tied to the act and process of incarnation as a sacred activity. It was more than just the transference of one's consciousness from one realm to another. It was in further exploring this quality of being a source and the process of incarnation itself that a number of insights and hypotheses arose, some of which are expressed in the premises I listed above, and all of which constitute the developing and emerging art of Incarnational Spirituality.

Incarnation

Since we're talking about an Incarnational Spirituality, how do I define "incarnation"? Let me start with a metaphor. Imagine an actor stepping onto a stage to participate in a play. As soon as she does so, she is in the play. But merely being onstage is not enough. She now needs to engage with and respond to the other actors on the stage, to the story that is unfolding, and to the audience who is watching.

There is more to being in a play than simply being present and onstage! A step to that engagement is to be aware of all the elements that are present that make up the production. These elements include the actor's own talents, past experience, knowledge of his or her lines, knowledge of the play, awareness of the audience and their needs, awareness of the other actors, and awareness of the props and set that are present on stage. The actor must connect to what is present through knowledge, instinct, craft, and senses. A failure to do so, such as ignorance of the placement of props on the set, can lead to an actor stumbling over something. A disconnection from the script can lead to an actor missing his cue or fumbling her lines.

Connection also means that the actor is in the right play. It means that she has not studied and practiced to be part of Hamlet and now discovers herself on the stage of Romeo and Juliet. It means she has what it takes to be connected to the play she is in. An actor can also be onstage and connected and engage in a limited way. By fulfilling the role he has been given, saying his lines when appropriate, moving about the stage as appropriate, speaking loudly enough to be heard, and so forth, he is doing his job. But in this case, he is not really a master of his craft. He doesn't bring something extra to the production, something uniquely his own. He is just doing what he is told to do in order to be part of the play and gets a paycheck.

An actor who really knows her craft, who reaches out to the other actors and enables them to shine and fulfill their roles more effectively, and who embraces the audience has charisma and presence. Such an actor, who brings herself into the role and gives it that added dimension of drama and reality, texture and presence, is someone who brings the whole event alive. She creates a wholeness in which fellow actors, the story, the audience, and the stage are all uplifted. Then the production achieves a level of coherency and wholeness that makes it more than just a play or an evening's entertainment. It becomes a deep experience. Something emerges that is more than just the story or the sets or the actors or the audience. I know I've had experiences in the theater when that has happened, and it has been remarkable. I've also seen productions where the actors are wooden and just going through the motions of the play, speaking the lines of dialog but not infusing any life or craft into the narrative. Boring!

One might describe the process here as:

• Being (one's presence on the stage - Embodiment),

• Connecting (being aware of the other actors, the props, the set, the audience, one's own training as an actor, etc.),

• Engaging (participating in the drama, interacting with the other actors, the set, the audience, bringing one's craft into play, etc.),

• Emergence (the overall gestalt of the play, the quality of the production, the energy that's generated and released for all involved.

Incarnation is usually seen as synonymous with Embodiment. To incarnate is to take on a body that enables you to be part of the realm in which you are incarnating. Certainly that is part of it, but it is not all of it, anymore than just being on stage is equivalent to taking part in the play. Just "Being" is not enough to be incarnated. More is required. Connection, Engagement, and Emergence represent that something extra. Incarnation, then, is a synthesis of Being, Connection, Engagement, and Emergence.

Being born puts us on the stage of this world. It gives us a body. Usually this is what is meant by incarnation. After all, the literal meaning of the word is "into flesh" or "into meat." But incarnation, in the context of Incarnational Spirituality, is much more than that, and in a broad sense, neither begins nor ends with our physical birth or our physical death. What I call the "incarnational round" includes a pre-birth state and a post-mortem state. That is a topic for another time

Even if we measure incarnation from physical birth to physical death, merely being in a physical body is only a part of incarnation. Equally important are the qualities of connection, engagement, and emergence. Incarnation is a process of connection, engagement, and emergence with the world. Like participating in a play, it is something we are doing all the time, not something that happened once when we entered on stage, with everything following being merely the working out of that initiating event. Furthermore, incarnation is creativity at work. It is a creative process and part of the larger creative process from which humanity, society, the earth, and the cosmos emerge.

When we participate in incarnation, we participate in our own unique way in the process by which all that is comes into being. One of the images that I use to symbolize incarnation is that of a chalice or cup. I think of incarnation as essentially a sacred act and I often image it as a grail. This is because a cup is a marriage of boundary and space, the finite and the infinite, both of which are necessary to manifest an identity in the form of a specific "domain of activity." Hold a cup in your hand and you can see this quite clearly.

The body of the cup, the rim, the container, is a specific boundary; it encloses a specific space, which is the volume of the cup. Put your finger inside the cup and wiggle it, then take your finger out and wiggle it in the air. It's the same space. Space is Space. But if I pour my coffee into the air, it will spill and splatter all over the place. The space in the air will not hold the coffee so I can drink it. If I pour the coffee into the cup, though, then the space will fill with coffee that is held and contained so that I can lift it to my lips and drink it.

With a boundary, (or a membrane, a definition, a limit, an edge), we define a space and give it an identity, which is often an identity of function. We give it the capacity to hold. What it holds depends on the specific nature of the boundary and the nature of our intent. What do we want it to hold?

Notes and Reflections

The Exercises

Each chapter includes exploratory exercises that constitute the practice (or "lab") side of the material and serve to illustrate the topic. Please try the exercise more than one time and record your experiences from each practice session in the space provided or in your personal journal. In Lorian's programs, much of the students' work revolves around doing exercises. Some of these exercises are like simple, mini-rituals; others are more reflective or contemplative. Some are intended to stimulate a particular kind of energy field around or within you, or connect you energetically with the world in a specific way. All are concerned with creating a state of mind and a felt sense within you.

An important element in doing these practices is a regular process for entering and leaving the state of mind that I metaphorically name "The Empty Stage". This exercise can be found on page 12. Within this process, you can do all the exercises I am proposing in this text. Consistency is a huge help in this kind of work. It builds coherency into what you do.

Beyond that, the exercises I offer are just suggestions. They are not cast in concrete. If you understand the purpose of the exercise, then you can feel free to redesign it and adapt it to your particular style and needs. Indeed, I encourage you to do so, so that you can enjoy the exercise as your own. An exercise is a living thing, filled with spirit, and it should blend with you in a way that honors and fosters your own spirit. In doing the exercise, it should emerge from you as much as from me and transform itself in any way that is needful in order for that to happen. It may contain elements that you may not wish to do or that seem too elaborate or just not your "style." All I ask is that you understand and honor the purpose behind the exercise and the spirit it is intended to embody. Then feel free to change it or adapt it, as you need.

To paraphrase Jesus, "You were not made for the exercises: the exercises are made to serve you."

Try each exercise at least once as presented, but please feel free after that to modify the form of the exercise to configure it to your unique needs and style. At the same time, be sure to retain the integrity of the basic objective and intent.

If at any time in doing an exercise, you feel any physical, mental, emotional, or psychic distress (this might feel like discomfort, tiredness, restlessness, or an intuitive sense of "No" about doing it or continuing to do it) stop immediately. Close the boundaries, ground yourself, and shift your attention and energies. You can change your attention completely by doing something physical to shift and change your energy. For example, do something fun that makes you laugh. This is an excellent way to change your energy.

Having to stop an exercise doesn't necessarily mean that you've come into contact with something dangerous or harmful. It is simply a sign that for some reason, that may or may not be evident, your energy in the moment is not or is no longer compatible with what you're doing. It may be a matter of timing, it may be that you are tired, or it may be that this exercise is not for you. As I said above, make the exercise your own. If need be, adjust it so you feel comfortable with it, or find a substitute.

In doing these exercises, the rule "no pain, no gain" most definitely does not apply!

Unless you have a strong inner sense not to do so, I would recommend trying the exercise one more time later. If the sense of disturbance or uneasiness continues, then clearly this exercise is not for you. Either change it or find some equivalent or simply skip it entirely.

Most of the exercises I suggest in this text have been used successfully by other people in the past. Some have emerged more recently from my work or have suggested by my own colleagues within the Inner Worlds.

Exercise One:
The Empty Stage

This is a generic practice for entering into a mild altered state and back again. It's highly adaptable. The main objective is to enter an open, evocative, imaginal space within which images and contacts may arise, and then to leave it again in an appropriate manner. Because I love theater, for me the image of an empty stage is very powerful and evocative. But you may find a different image more potent for you. Please feel free to experiment. It's the state of evocative receptivity we're after, not a particular setting or image.

Entering the theater with the empty stage is a form of shifting from everyday awareness into a particular kind of altered consciousness oriented to inner journeys and working with imaginal states. In essence, it is a more elaborate form of lighting a candle!

1. Take time to relax and quiet your mind, your feelings, and your body.

2. Imagine that there is a threshold in front of you. This can take any form you wish, but the most natural may be the form of a door or portal that you will step through as you cross the threshold. This door is closed at first. Open it. If you feel the need, you can imagine guardians or allies standing on either side, protecting the door and threshold and protecting you as well.

3. Cross over the threshold. If you wish and if it will make you feel safe, you can imagine a guardian or ally crossing over with you.

4. You enter a theater. It is the theater of your heart and mind, the place of your imagination. It is a place of daydreams, fantasies, visualizations, images, and stories. You are standing at the back of the theater. In front of you are rows of theater seats and an empty stage. Go forward and sit in one of the seats in any of the rows. Look around and be aware of the theater around you, hushed and expectant for what may appear on stage.

5. In front of you is an empty stage, an empty space. Feel the

evocative, creative power of this space. Anything can take shape there. Any story could be told on that stage, any characters or settings could manifest upon it. Feel its imaginative power. Feel the wonder and anticipation at what might appear on this empty stage, this open space of potential and invocation. Appreciate its possibilities.

6. If you are doing an imaginative exercise, then it begins here at this step. Something appropriate to the exercise will appear on the stage and draw you into it. You will find yourself on the stage, the theater disappearing, and yourself immersed in the imaginal world of the exercise. When the exercise is complete, you will find yourself back on the stage, which is once again empty. You will again step down and find a seat in the audience where you will be energized, filled with grace and blessed.

7. Once you have a felt sense of this empty stage and its open, evocative, creative space, get up and go back out of the theater the way you came. Cross back through the door over the threshold into your everyday normal surroundings and your everyday, normal consciousness. Any guardians that went with you into the theater come back out and take up their posts by the door into the theater.

8. Give thanks for whatever you have received and for any allies or beings who assisted you. Give thanks to your inner theater of your heart and mind. Feel any energies that remain with you from being in the theater grounding themselves into your body if they feel positive or being released to the light and transformative power of your guardians or to the spirit of the sacred if they feel unsettling or negative. Feel the power of your own Light rising within you, gracefully integrating you back into the energies and fields of your daily life, but with full awareness of any blessings you have received from your experiences in the theater. As you feel comfortable and ready, go about your daily life.

Take some time to repeat this exercise, moving in and out of your theater, feeling the nature of that shift, and gaining a felt sense of the evocative, creative power of the empty stage. When you need to, you will be able to go directly to that felt sense and into that creative open space as a result of practicing this exercise.

Notes and Reflections

11/8 - I know I was doing something on stage but I can't remember what!

Exercise Two: Creating a Boundary

Here's a simple exercise. In the middle of your living room floor, designate an area that you will call "magical" or "sacred," and use some means to differentiate it from the rest of the floor. You might take thread, for instance, and lay it down in a circle. Or you might take four candles and place them down at each of the cardinal points of east, south, west, and north just outside of that designated space. Or you could use pillows, books, or anything else to set the space off from the rest of the floor. Now physically there is no difference between the floor within the circle and the floor outside the circle (I'm making an assumption here about the nature and condition of your living room floor!). But yet, there is a difference. Part of the floor is within a boundary and part of it is not. The boundary creates a differential, and this differential is at the heart of all energy flow, all creativity, and all activity.

Think for a moment of weather. Winds blow because of differentials in temperature and pressure between one region and another. Normally, we can't see those differences. A person usually can't look into the sky and see where pressure changes or temperature changes or even where wind is, if we don't see something blowing. (These are potential problems at airports when pilots cannot see wind shear conditions that can damage a place.) But these differentials are very real boundaries or membranes or lines of difference that create energy and activity.

Likewise, the significant boundary you've created in your living room. You can even do this without using any props like candles, threads or anything that can be seen with the naked eye. It can be experienced, just as one can experience wind. In some ways, the threads, candles or whatever you've used to designate where the boundary is, is like a windsock that tells you where the wind is and what direction it's blowing. But because we are tangible, physical, particular beings, having something to designate the boundary is useful.

Anyway, now you need to determine the nature of this boundary. Say to yourself (and picture it in your imagination) that the space inside the boundary is a "magical" or "sacred" space where special spiritual or magical energy is invoked. "See" in your mind's eye a column of

Light, let's say, that fills this space within the boundary you've created. Now step across the boundary into this space. Do you feel a difference? What is that difference like? Step back and forth across the boundary. Do it with your eyes open and with your eyes closed. Stand inside the boundary and invoke spirit and Light and energy in whatever way is familiar and comfortable to you and feel that spirit or light or spirit filling that space. When you have this felt sense, step out of the circle again. What does that feel like? How does the rest of the living room feel compared to the space within the boundary? What you feel will depend in part on your own native sensitivity to energy.

You may feel an intense, tangible difference, or you may feel nothing at all (in which case you can try again later or create an entirely different exercise). If you do feel something, and most people do (though there can be quite appropriate and valid reasons why you may not, so don't at all think you've failed in some way if you don't) think about the significance of this. Why would you feel a difference? What is the nature of the boundary? Do you honestly believe that some threads, candles or pillows or whatever you used to designate the boundary could confine spirit or Light or blessing or a subtle, non-physical energy? Yet, it <u>can</u> be confined and held in just this way.

Before we move on, we need to restore your living room to its former condition. That's easily done. Give thanks to the space you created and the energies it contained. Then imagine or see in your mind's eye the boundary dissolving and all that good energy radiating out into the world. Pick up the thread, remove the candles, do whatever is necessary to remove the boundary so that your living room is back to the way it was before you started the exercise. Be sure to record your experiences with this exercise on the next pages or in your personal journal.

Notes and Reflections

Chapter Two:
More On Incarnation

In the "Creating a Boundary" exercise which you have just completed obviously, what is holding the column of Light (the structure of the cup, so to speak) is itself non-physical and energetic; it is imaginal. It is partly that you have identified and named that space in a way differently than you named the rest of the living room. You have, in effect, incarnated a space of Light and energy and blessing. We do this all the time with altars, sacred spaces, medicine circles, and the like. We do it as well with so-called ordinary spaces. It doesn't take a great deal of psychic power to discern the difference in energy in different rooms of a house. There's an old poem that says it well: "No matter where I put my guests, they seem to like my kitchen best!" Now of course, there can be quite good physical reasons for liking a kitchen best. It's where food is. It's often the warmest room in the house, which is nice on cold days. But it's also because it's probably the room where the most activity takes place and energy invoked. It is a lived-in room, filled within human energy, to which we are attracted. Yet the physical space in the kitchen is no different from the physical space in any other room. I mean the quality of "space-ness," not necessarily how the space is filled and arranged, decorated and maintained.

Let's go back to your cup. A cup contains the same space that is in the air around you, yet it's a different space. It has an identity, just as the sacred circle you created in your living room has an identity. If you drop a cup and smash it, the space it contained doesn't disappear. It's where it always was, but now it's become indistinguishable from all the other space around you. In addition, there is an interesting phenomenon. You may still feel the echo of that energy, particularly in the part of the room where you had your special space. Partly this is because you have sensitized that area (and now, by releasing its energy into the room and beyond, the room itself). This sensitivity will wear away over time. Notice what would happen though if you created a magical space there everyday in the same place and in the same or equivalent way. There would then come a time when the column of light or energy differential or presence of energy would stabilize and become a relatively permanent part of the room, whether the boundary was there or not. Likewise, I hope you can see that you don't actually have to do anything physical to create this boundary and establish this space, at least not in this instance. In some ways, it's simply a choice. Well, there's a bit more to it than that from an Incarnational Spirituality point of view. I can say, "I am entering this room as if I were entering a sacred space" and behave accordingly. Or I can say, "Ho hum, this is just an ordinary space; it's my living room" or "it's the bus station" or "it's the employment office" or "it's my cubicle at work."

How I enter the space, how I inhabit it, how I incarnate into it, will make a difference. Of course, there is a difference between a bus station and a cathedral. There is (usually!) a difference in architecture and furnishings and decoration, all of which have an effect. But the space within a bus station is still the same space as within a cathedral. Part of what makes one space different energetically from the other is intent and expectation. There is no reason whatsoever that I cannot enter a bus station, the employment office, or my cubicle and expect, intend, and inhabit it as a sacred space. I could make it as much a sacred space as a cathedral. Now in such an instance, the sacredness of the space will configure to the boundaries and nature of the space itself. I will most likely express sacredness or spirituality in a cathedral (through worship or prayer or meditation or song) in a different way than I may in a bus station, employment office or my work cubicle. In the latter, I might express sacredness through honoring those around me with respect, courtesy, a loving or non-adversarial attitude, and so on). It can still be a sacred space with sacred energies. So invoking and inhabiting (incarnating) sacred space is one of the skills or capacities that we work with in Incarnational Spirituality. It is a perfectly normal, perfectly accessible human capacity that does not require extraordinary skills or developments of spirituality.

Here is another characteristic of incarnation: it is the capacity of creating and inhabiting a specific space. Or put another way, incarnation is the art of making cups. It is the process of generating a specific, particular bounded space. It is also an art of holding.

At the center of this process is the Generative Mystery, which is expressing itself through love and the capacity of the will-to-be. This Mystery is at the heart of all incarnation. Immediately around it are four functions: Identity, Boundary, Relationship, and Emergence. These are equivalent to the four functions we listed above when talking about the actor on stage: Being, Connection, Engagement, and Emergence.

The creation of boundaries that create a space in which a specific activity of identity can take place (or in which a particular identity can manifest) can also be seen as a form of connection, since we connect through our boundaries and across the energy differentials between us. Connection and engagement can both be subsumed under "Relationship." Engagement can also be equated with Relationship. The point is that we see a gestalt of a four-fold expression. This expression has result of expressing, in a specific way, a unique identity that can relate to, partner and co-create with, and be co-generative with other unique identities. This in turn allows new identity to emerge. This gestalt of activity is the holism of incarnation.

Let's think of incarnation as the creation of a unique space. I call the space within a boundary an "identity of activity." That is, the space has particular configurations based on its boundaries or its defining characteristics. My house is a space bounded by its walls and internally divided into various sections. The activity of this space (the identity of this space) is defined as a "place to live." I could also use the metaphor of a coffee cup, but that would be mess! Just pouring coffee into the space of the house results in stained carpets, dirty floors, and a necessity to lap up my coffee from the floor like a cat. Not what I want to do first thing in the morning! But a coffee cup provides an "identity of activity" that is uniquely suited to holding and giving me my coffee in a tasteful way.

However, I couldn't live in my coffee cup. This is all very obvious. The point I want to make, though, is that the space within the house and within the coffee cup and within the Puget Sound bioregion (bounded on all four directions by mountains) is the same space. It is the boundaries that define these spaces that are all different, giving them unique identities and capacities. They can be "used" or are suitable for different activities. One holds coffee, one holds a home, and one holds cities, towns and a bioregion. But the overall incarnational principles behind each of them are the same: there is identity, boundary and holding, connection and engagement, and emergence. I like to use the term "identity of activity" because it reminds me that I am an identity that is also an activity; I am a noun and a verb, a particle and a wave. There is nothing static about incarnation or the incarnate state. Every being, no matter on what level it functions, is in an incarnate state. The cosmos is an incarnate state. But it's also a clumsy term that can sound like jargon, so we will only use it to evoke this sense of activity and process, flow and motion. It's just a fun definition that we can take or leave, as we need.

However, it may help me to conceive of myself as a unique space of activity. I normally think of myself as a person, which is a kind of thing or object: a particle. But I can also see myself as a space, just as the circle on your living room floor created a space. I am a space generated and created by my soul in order to carve out room within the overall space of the world within which a particular kind of activity (part of which is called "David Spangler") can take place. The space that I am is created by boundaries. There are many of these boundaries or edges that create a differential between what I am and the environment is. The most obvious one at a physical level is our skin, but we have energetic, psychological, and spiritual structures that act as boundaries as well. These boundaries are part of our incarnation and they function not only to create a space but also to create difference. In a way, we act like weather. The difference between you and me stimulates energy that flows between us. Note that this flow can take on qualities that make it loving or hurtful, compassionate or violent, and so forth. Essentially the flow itself is neutral and open to being conditioned or qualified by what we do and think and feel.

Now a space is an area in which an activity can take place. What are these activities? Well, to some extent, this is determined by the nature of the boundaries. A strainer that holds my loose tea leaves provides a different kind of boundary and thus a different activity than the teacup that holds the hot water and the strainer, allowing the tea to brew. Spaces can be very versatile. For example, the space created by a coffee cup can be used for a variety of things other than holding coffee. I have a wonderful coffee cup that I actually use to store my pens and pencils. It has a wonderful illustration on it, and I decided I'd rather have it as a decoration on my desk than drink coffee from it and risk it being broken in our dishwasher. I use cups to hold and shake dice in some games, as something to store marbles and buttons in, as a holder for soup, and as a mock hole with which to practice golf putting.

In a similar way, the "space" that is each of us is also amazingly versatile. It can hold our everyday thoughts and feelings; it can hold our memories and our personal sense of self. It can also hold energies. It can hold another person (as in "I hold you in my heart," which esoterically is much more than just a metaphor). It can hold imagination. It can hold images of what has never been or of what hasn't been yet but could be. It can hold spirit. It can hold the sacred.

I can shrink the space of myself right down to a small, constrained, fearful, hateful, angry ball of hurt and pain or expand myself into a space so large that the cosmos could fit into it. It can hold a space of love, imagination, hope, wonder, and expanded energy. I can say, "My space is only large enough to hold the people who are in my family, or people like me." I can say, "My space can hold Jews but not Arabs, Christians but not Moslems." I can also expand my space to hold all peoples. The point is that I control my space. I can expand it or limit it. I am fundamentally a shape changer. We all are.

Shape change, in this sense, may not be easy. I may have to overcome and alter boundaries I have taken on from parents, culture, and history, but it is still possible. That is the power of incarnation. Incarnation is the capacity and power to create and form shapes, because incarnation is a shape.

The whole objective of Incarnational Spirituality is to learn to understand and "control" (I use the term "inhabit") this space-changing, space-creating ability in ways that will bless and positively affect the space of the world (the incarnation of the world) around us. That, ultimately, is what Incarnational Spirituality is all about.

Let's go back to our metaphor of the actors and the stage. I said that from my point of view, incarnation is not the same as embodiment. Embodiment gives me a physical body. Birth is about embodiment. Incarnation begins at a much earlier stage at the level of the soul and involves extending an identity that will connect and engage with the earth and hold a space in a particular way so that something (really, many things) may emerge. So I might say that I incarnate into a play when I sign on as an actor to be part of it. Ahead of me are rehearsals and all the processes of training, costuming, working with the director and producer and other actors, and all the other things that go in to getting the play ready for opening night. When the curtain goes up and I step onto the stage, I am now embodied into the play that now includes the audience. The audience is part of that embodiment, a final connection I must make to be part of the play as a piece of theater and not just as a private production for a group of set designers, costumers and actors. To be fully incarnated, I need to connect and engage with the actors, the set, and the audience.

There is a quality of mindfulness about incarnation. But there are degrees to this connection and engagement. I can just run through my lines and move about the stage and play my role and that's it. This way of being connected is neither inspired nor inspirational. I can also choose to delve deeply into my craft and really put myself into the role and the drama, working co-creatively with the other actors and with the audience to make a fully alive, fully fleshed out performance. In doing so, I am mindful of and in service to not only my own performance and well being but that of my fellow actors. How can I help them succeed? How can I enable their best performances to come out? How can I help the audience to appreciate and applaud all of us, not just me in some narcissistic way? How can I serve the intent of the play, the power of theater, the spirit of drama as it flows through the whole system, the whole gestalt, of the production, which embraces audience, all the actors, the musicians (if any), and the sets on stage?

Put in terms of incarnational spirituality, how can my incarnation become a blessing to the incarnations of all whom I meet, of all around me, or at least of those with whom I engage in a daily way? Here I touch on a mystery of space. The space in the cup is the space in the house is the space in the biosphere is the space in the planet. How can the use of a particular space honor the spaceness within all spaces? The space within my coffee cup, as "space" is capable of holding the entire world, all the cosmos, not at a level of phenomena or quantity, but as a quality, as "spaceness." This is just a metaphor, of course, but when we speak of ourselves, it becomes much less a metaphor and more a reality.

My unique incarnation is one with the process (the "space") of incarnation itself. My unique space has the capacity to hold the essence, or wholeness, of all space. This is the secret of my sacredness. To fully appreciate this, I need to not think in terms of quantity or measurement; I have to think in terms of quality and presence. Each of us has the capacity to hold in our incarnations through a presence of love (a presence perfectly accessible to each of us) the cosmos as a whole, or at least that part of the cosmos that we meet and engage with everyday. We can hold it in a way that enables it to be a more capable of holding space as well. We can hold others in our hearts, minds, and energy in ways that foster and bless the fullest capacities of their incarnations. Isn't that what spirituality is all about?

I was soaking in the bathtub, always a Good Place for attunement, and began to thinking some more about the cup metaphor and also the need for something concrete to ground this material with. Some ideas popped into my mind from the Bathtub Deva (the one that always gives us our best ideas in Bathtubs and Showers, and encourages us to sing in them, too, where we inevitably sound operatic <grin >), so here they are. Nothing like squeezing every bit of juice from an image, otherwise what's a meta-phor? Hee hee.

So imagine that two cooperative intelligences inhabit a cup. One is the intelligence of the cup itself, whose function is to be a boundary, enclose a space, and create specificity and particularity. The other is the intelligence of the space itself. Its function is to hold. What it holds is a co-creative function and partnership with the cup. Space can hold a sun but Cup cannot. Space plus Cup can hold liquids, buttons, pencils, or coins. But let's not limit Cup. Let's say that the "Intelligence of Cup" is that of any structure that sets boundaries, encloses space, and creates specificity. So Cup could be a house, a bioregion, a planet, a '64 Impala, a box, ad infinitum. Cup can take many forms, including a cauldron, a grail, and a womb. It could even be a skull or brain. But whatever form Cup takes, it sets boundaries, it differentiates, it provides for a space (or a condition of activity). It creates specificity. Even if the Cup is the Cosmos, it's still <u>this</u> cosmos with its particular universal constants that allow a particular kind of physics and chemistry to exist which in turn allow a particular kind of life and consciousness to exist and manifest. Cup is powerful. But Cup serves Space. It Incarnates Space. Space is the Intelligence of Holding, of Love, of Roominess, of Spaciousness, of Possibility, of Growth and Evolution, of Emergence.

Space is powerful.

Together they form an incarnation, infinite forms of incarnation. Cup provides particularity, but Space provides universality. An incarnation has both. The intelligence of Cup says, "This, specifically, is what I am. Here are my boundaries at the moment. I am the Intelligence of Individuality." The intelligence of Space says, "I can hold all things and in me all things can become. I am the Identity that permits all identities to be. I am the Intelligence of Self, of Being. The Cup of me has the function of allowing David Spangler to exist and thus manifests as a whole variety of interlocking, nested cups: physical body, mind, memories, likes, dislikes, and so forth. Also, the content within one cup can become a cup for still more particularized content. Thus the "Cup of Brain" becomes a Cup for Mind which can in turn become a Cup for Memories which can become a Cup for Specific Memory of something I like, or dislike, and so on. Or we can say that all the particularizing functions that give me a singular identity as David are summed up in the function and intelligence of Cup. The Space of me, however, allows David to not become a closed system, limited or bound only to the dimensions of the Cup. The Space of me can hold others, hold imagination, hold the world around me, hold God, hold my friends, hold my enemies, and hold the cosmos.

The difference between you and me is not in our Space. We share Space. The same intelligence of Space is in both of us. For that matter, the same intelligence of Cup is in both of us, too. We both can hold. The function of Cup creates significant and important differences between us, and those differences can generate the "weather" of creativity or conflict or elements of both between us. It allows a very specific and dynamic Cup of Relationship to emerge between us which will not be the same as the Cup of Relationship we have with anyone else. The Cup part of us is not hard to experience.

The Space part of us is tricky. This is because I may think of my unique space as limited, when in fact it's not so much limited as particularized because of Cup and presumed certain powers due to that particularization. But the Intelligence of Space within me can "think" with the Intelligence of Space within a tree. This allows for a sense of oneness with a tree while simultaneously recognizing and honoring that a tree isn't me and I'm not a tree. We can lose a sense of our own Space or the Intelligence of Space because we see vast Space, Big Space, outside of us and call it God, the Sacred, Spirit, the World, the Other, and so on. But some of that vastness we see is not Space but Big Cups. The World IS a Big Cup compared to me. But our Space is the same. So when I go into my identity and intelligence as Space, I can just as easily be the Space that is the sacred, the Space that is within the world, the space that is within the cosmos, the space that is within an ant, the space that is within anything. I can't hold their content as they do. That capacity is their specific gift of holding born of their partnership with Cup. But I can share the power of Holding.

That is part of what I mean by being sacred, by being a source. It isn't that God is within us as a Big Space or Big Cup. It's that when I step into my "Intelligence of Space," I am simply Space and I can partner with whatever Cup I am capable of partnering with to create a specific kind of holding. Please note here a concept that is VERY important to Incarnational Spirituality. I am not JUST Space.

We like to think and are sometimes taught that what we really, truly, authentically are is Spirit or something transcendental or beyond form or part of a Oneness, but that is often just saying that we are really a BIG Space defined by a BIG Cup. What we authentically are is Cup + Space, or that which can manifest as both Cup and Space. An analogy is Light that is said in quantum physics to manifest as both Particle and Wave. We are the Intelligence that can hold and particulate, that can be Cup and Space. This, to me, is the Intelligence of Incarnation. So my Space can partner with your Cup, which is just another way of saying that I can honor, respect, love, and work co-creatively with your uniqueness, your difference from me, your self and identity. And if we can be Space to each other's Cups and Cups to each other's Space, then a new Cup and Space emerges between us which can hold what neither of us could hold.

Here's a concrete example: When I was younger before I had children, I imagined that I had a deep understanding of love. But a lot of what I knew as love was a spiritual love arising from mystical experiences I had had. When I partnered with Julie, in the relationship between us, I experienced depths and characteristics of love that I hadn't known. Then when our first child, John-Michael, was born, suddenly the first night he came home from the hospital, I was suddenly plunged into a sense of partnership and love, into a Cup and Space, I had not known. It was even more encompassing than that which I had with Julie. For unlike Julie who was a fully capable, adult person, John-Michael was wholly dependent upon me. He pulled out layers of responsibility and accountability in my loving that went beyond what I had with Julie. That's how I think of it in hindsight, of course. At the time, I just felt like I had fallen into a bottomless chasm of love unlike what I had known before. A space opened betwixt my children and me unlike any of the spaces that had opened amid others and me. This is not at all an unusual experience. I imagine most parents know exactly what I'm talking about. I'm just putting it in this context of Cups and Spaces.

Space to me is neither passive nor simply receptive. It partners with what it holds and creates for everything it holds the potential of spaciousness. This potential invites and allows for growth. What's space for if we can't grow into it? Let's go back to our actor metaphor for a moment. The skilled actor, who is plying her craft in a manner that heightens and enables all the other actors to do better in their craft as well, is a person uniting her Space with theirs and with their Cups. In her Space is the dynamic energy of "THEATER" and "ACTING" and all those concepts make possible. As a Cup, she is just one single actor on stage. In her Space, she can be all actors throughout time, all united in the beauty and power of the Craft of Theater. At the same time, she can be the other actors around her in this specific play (which is its own kind of Cup), helping them all inhabit and incarnate (live in and out from) the Space of that play. Simultaneously, she is helping all of them share her experience of the Space of Acting and Theater.

In Incarnational Spirituality terms, she is acting as an Agent of Incarnation, someone whose mindful presence in the moment enhances and enables the incarnations of others. In Cup/Space terms, she enhances the Intelligence of Cup and Space around her through how she inhabits and incarnates her own Intelligence of Cup and Space. We can speak of this phenomenon as Love and Inspiration and let it go at that. I think we can tweak out a fuller understanding of the incarnational forces involved, of our Cupness and Spaceness and how they interact and thereby inhabit this Agency, this Lovingness, even more mindfully.

So I seek the ability to partner with others and with my world in a way that enhances the potential for spaciousness, uniqueness, growth, being, holding, boundaries, connections, engagement, and emergence. That is the objective of Incarnational Spirituality. And it's one I feel is perfectly accessible by any of us. Why don't I just call this "Love" in action, when obviously that is one way of understanding this process? I think it's because we have used the word "Love" so much and so often in spiritual contexts that it ceases to have meaning. It is muffled and bound in familiarity and expectation. It's what we expect to hear from a spiritual teacher. So it doesn't grab us by the throat and shake us with its exuberance and joy, and awaken us. It doesn't make us proud to be who we are as individual selves, and make us partners with God and Cosmos, and make us delight in the differences of others...all the things that Love does.

The word love can frighten us with visions of Olympian spiritual feats of agape and forgiveness and lovingness and unity and oneness. Do any of you remember when Pope John-Paul II went to the prison and forgave the man who tried to assassinate him? Do you remember how it was played up in the media as a tremendous, unusual, fantastic event, as evidence of the spirituality of the Pope? Not to belittle the power and glory of the Pope's forgiveness, but from a spiritual point of view, it was as natural and ordinary as one person kissing another was. Imagine if we lived in a world where the sight of one person hugging another in friendship, or simply shaking hands, caused banner headlines around the world as if something so far beyond ordinary human experience had taken place that we could only stand stunned before it? Yet, that's how we treated the Pope forgiving his would-be killer, for doing something that all of us should do as naturally as breathing. Yet we know from experience that forgiveness can be hard, that love is hard...but part of that is because we make it hard. We treat acts of love, kindness, and forgiveness as exceptions to the ordinary, as signs of spiritual greatness, as something "evolved" souls do but not something the rest of us do. Thus we either disempower the word love or we overly empower it. It becomes too familiar so we think we know what a person is saying when he says, Love one another. Conversely, it becomes too difficult to love so we shy away and make excuses when a person says Love one Another. We say, "well, that would be nice in an ideal world, but in the REAL world..." What REAL world is that? So I tend to shy away from talking about Love and ask folks to think in different ways to accomplish the same ends.

If I invite you to encounter your Self, your Individuality, as a Cup and Space, that is an unusual perspective. I want to suggest that the function of Cup and the function of Space are the same for you, God, and me. It's a lot for the mind and heart to grasp that when we perform those functions. I am being you, you are being God, God is being me, I am being me, you are being you, God is being God, you are being me, God is being you, and I am being God, Simultaneously we are all being ourselves and different. It's really very simple. In Incarnational Spirituality, I conceive of God (because this is how I experience the Sacred, not because I'm particularly philosophically inclined or smart) as configuring to Cup and Space. So when my Cup-Space, my personality, can hold in a loving way the chair I'm sitting in and nothing else (rather like Archie Bunker, that long ago TV character who said "that's as far as my 'love-muscles' can take me"), I am still performing a sacred act. God is not saying, "Can't you be more loving? If you were really loving, you would love everything, or at least everything in your neighborhood." God is celebrating fully what my Cup and Space can hold. God lives in the Holding not in the extent or quantity of how much is held.

It's for this reason that I invite us to honor our personalities and personal selves and individual identities and selfness as well as our transpersonal or spiritual or "sacred" or vast or unified Selves. The size of the Cup and Space doesn't matter. The mindfulness and quality of the Holding does. The personality is fundamentally an instrument for Holding, a Cup that provides a Space. The Cup of Personhood, of incarnate, personal identity gives us access to, connection with, and engagement with, the particularity and specificity of this world in which we live. What a miracle that we can stand in this world as a self in the midst of other selves! What power! What spaciousness we can bring to each other and the world! What creativity we can generate! God had a Very Good Idea when God made us! Whatever origin myth and perspective you'd like to use, it was a good thing! Huzzah! Let's raise our Cups to good Ideas!

Being an Agent of Incarnation

OK, having gotten Cup and Space out of my system, for now

anyway, let me see if I have anything here for those practically inclined.

I thought, while soaking in the bathtub, that one approach would be to describe how I use Incarnational Spirituality in practical ways in the course of my life, say in the course of a day. This would be by way of providing a concrete example of Incarnational Spirituality at work.

Now I should say that I have some resistance to doing this because I believe that each person discovers how to do Incarnational Spirituality uniquely in his or her own life. I don't consider myself a model of how it's done. In any event, the nature of my life and the work I do makes my daily regime not entirely the usual. I'm still a human person engaging with all the challenges and joy with which we all deal, so I think sharing my personal experiences may help, as long as it doesn't overly concretize the material. I have to say that my way of teaching for nearly fifty years has been to state general principles and then let people discover for themselves how to specifically apply them in their own daily lives. So this is a bit of an experiment for me. For me, Incarnational Spirituality is not a philosophy; it is a practice. It's not "THE" practice, heaven forbid, and it's not a practice that cannot be added to or combined with other elements of spiritual practice coming from other traditions such as Christianity or Buddhism.

The objective of the practice is to be an "agent of incarnation" in the ways I've described above. In effect, this is the 7th Premise listed earlier. An agent of incarnation is simply a person who mindfully uses the presence of his or her own incarnational process (the Cup and Space) to serve the incarnational process (or processes) all around him or her. How can I enable a person I meet or a thing I encounter to be more fully incarnate than it was before? Now if I just think of incarnation as having a form or a body, then this question doesn't make a lot of sense. It's like asking, "How can I enable my wife to have more of a body than she has now?" [Well, I suppose I could feed her chocolates and milkshakes, but that's not what I have in mind here.] It's not a bigger body but more bodiness, which as I say, does not make any sense on a physical level.

If I feel a person is somewhat spacey in his or her life and "not all here," as they say, I suppose I could interpret this question to mean, "How can I enable this person to be more present in their body, more aware of their surroundings and of themselves?" That's getting closer to what I mean. I use the example of the actor who uses her craft to enable other actors to act even more fully, more connectedly, in a more engaged manner and more open to emergence than before. This example puts me in the ballpark of what I mean by the practice of being an Agent of Incarnation. In simplest terms, how can I radiate the energy of incarnation in such a way that another person's capacities of identity and being, boundaries, connection and engagement, and emergence are enhanced?

Now just what that means in a practical way is very situational. It could mean many things. It means something different if I'm connecting and engaging with a person than if I'm connecting and engaging with an object. And yes, I have a shamanic worldview and experience that everything (and I mean everything) in the world around me is alive and has presence. I do not believe that everything has an empersonal spirit, as I understand that term, because not everything has a personal identity that results from a mindful and willed act of incarnation.

The energy that forms the empersonal spirit emerges in part from the presence of will and intent. So my sofa did not will itself to be a sofa and thus has no empersonal spirit as such, but it is alive. It does possess an energy field, and it can be aware of and respond to other energy fields in its environment. Of course, it doesn't have biological life, but the assumption that life can only be biological is a bias and rather quaintly limited from a shamanic perspective! Even if I did not experience everything as being alive, I would still wish to meet and treat everything with honor and respect for its "isness," for its beingness, which even if I don't experience it in the particular form, I may experience in its sacred form.

So for example, in Buddhism there is the teaching of the "isness" of things, the "isness" of a sofa, the "isness" of a chair, or the "isness" of a stone. In Christianity, this is not a major or familiar perspective (often quite the opposite). But I can still understand all things as being embraced in the love and beingness of God, so to be kind to my sofa can still be considered as being kind to an aspect of the whole that is part of God.

Actually, this idea of being an agent of incarnation and of the radiant nature of incarnation as being a divine presence, and not just an act, is part of a cosmology and understanding of sacredness that is more than I can get into here. The first five Premises all relate to that cosmology and understanding.

OK, so, are we getting practical and down-to-earth yet? Ha! With that objective as an overall meaning and purpose of Incarnational Spirituality, I enter my day. Ta da! Sometime in the first hour of so of my day, I take a moment of alignment. I don't have a regular ritual for this that I do everyday, but in some manner, I honor and give thanks for my incarnation, for my personal self, for the connections I have to the world, for the world itself, for the presence of the Sacred. In short, I take a moment to see myself as an agent of incarnation, a potential partner to all whom I meet and all the things I engage with, partnering with them in our shared incarnational process. I remind myself that my purpose this day is to enhance my world however I can. I have no huge, messianic thoughts about this. I'm not trying to affect the whole world. I just want to be mindful in going about my business that I do so in the midst of life and living beings, all of whom seek fulfillment in their own lives and incarnations, all of whom seek happiness, flow, and the experience of the sacred. Often this is just a moment of reminding and a moment of standing, as per the exercise. I consciously connect and align my "Cupness," my incarnational particularity, with the cupness of all around me. I quite consciously affirm and give thanks for the gift of particularity, for the gifts that boundaries bring, for the differences that surround me. And I consciously connect my Space, my interiority and felt sense of spaciousness, with the Space (and spaces) all around me. I go into the felt sense that the Space I am holds all the cosmos because holding is the nature of that function within me, and as Space, there is no limit to its Holding. This prepares me to hold in my heart and mind and energy whatever I meet this day. It prepares me to be loving.

This whole process may only take a few minutes. It's really entering into a felt sense of being a source, of being generative, of being a point of radiance for my world, not simply as some transpersonal being inside a body but as a personality, as a body, as a human particle, a human self. Now, this puts me into a certain frame of mind; it organizes my energy in a particular way. I'm not sure how else to describe it. I have an expectation for what I'm about to meet. Some days I awaken tired or not feeling well or distracted, and after attuning to my capacity to hold, I just hold those feelings. I honor them and hold them. I don't try to fight them; I don't try to rise above them. I don't see them as an impediment or an obstruction to my spirit, my Cupness, my Space-ness, my love, my incarnation. They are only what I'm starting my day holding. Whatever I hold is held in sacredness; that is the heart of this practice. And I find that even if the tiredness or the aches or the worry or whatever it is doesn't go away, it changes its character. It's energy changes. I do not identify with its "charge" or its energy, so it cannot possess me. And if I do so identify with it and it does possess me, then I witness that and hold that. I don't say, "Oh, that is what personalities do! That is how the personality or the ego gets in the way by clinging to negativity or fear."

My understanding of my personality through the work I've done with Incarnational Spirituality is that it is nothing more or less than a function that particularizes. And in this case I am particularizing negativity. My personality is doing what it should. It is presenting me with an opportunity to connect and engage with negative feelings that are present in the world. It is giving me an opportunity to participate in feelings that grip the majority of humanity. It's painful and distracting but why would I want to avoid it, if I can give service by holding these feelings and acknowledging them? I don't seek out negativity just in order to be "one of the guys", so to speak, but when it comes, I hold it. You could say I take it into my identity, but in a way that changes it. Simply because I'm not fighting it, I'm not using the negativity to tell myself a story about how bad or unworthy or unspiritual I am or as a club with which to beat myself. I become like Teflon to its charge. It can be held, but it doesn't attach like a parasite. This is the power of active holding; what I hold with mindfulness doesn't attach (well, usually not! ahem...)

And if I also understand that the power to hold is a sacred act in itself, then by holding, I am bringing what I hold into the presence of the Sacred. This is worthy of a class all by itself! So I begin my day by in effect attuning to myself and to my incarnation, by standing, and in this way I also attune to the presence of Self, Incarnation, and the Sacred in macro terms. Then I go about my work. Now in my case that usually means long sessions at the computer either writing text for classes or working on a book or some other project. But in the morning, I may first be involved in cooking breakfast for my kids, getting them off to school (my two daughters have to catch buses to their respective schools by 7AM in the morning). Or if I have a good flow and want to begin writing immediately, Julie takes over the household tasks, which, I must admit, is what happens most mornings, as I do my best writing in the morning.

How do you cook eggs or pancakes in an Incarnational Spirituality way? I guess the same way you would ordinarily, except, I suppose, with a sense of pleasure and engagement with the physicality and particularity of the task. That is part of what Incarnational Spirituality means to me, a celebration of the particular, of the small miracles and things of life, like making pancake batter or toast or cooking an egg. Also, when I greet my sons and daughters as they come out (I'm usually the first one up in our household, sometimes getting up by 4:30 or 5 am- but not always!), I do so in a particular way. That is, when I see them, I honor them as fellow incarnate beings. That doesn't sound like much...of course they are fellow incarnate beings. But for me, that they are both unique particular persons and that they are the presence of the cosmos is something to celebrate and wonder at. I can feel myself honoring their uniqueness—their Cupness—and I can feel my Space reaching out to greet and blend with their Space.

This probably sounds all mystical and spiritual, but the felt sense of it is quite different. As I have attuned over the years to the felt sense of Incarnation as a function, I've developed a felt sense of being surrounded by Incarnation, like a fish is surrounded by water. In some ways, I experience other people as specific nodes or eddies or currents or energy fields within that water (talk about mixing metaphors). This is a tangible, energetic experience for me. Here is where I still have some difficulty with perception, for there are things I have perceived all my life that I still discover others do not perceive. These things seem concrete and tangible to me, but to others they are abstract and mystical. Not much I can do about that except to be aware of it. So part of my problem in this example is to separate what I do that comes from practicing Incarnational Spirituality and what Incarnational Spirituality is because of what I experience and do anyway given my particular sensitivities. Did the fact that I see people as coalescences of a universal energy or function I call Incarnation lead to some of what I teach as Incarnational Spirituality, or do I see people that way because I've been research and working with Incarnational Spirituality for several years?

I don't fully know, but much of it is the first reason, not the second.

Still, what is important is that whatever I do with or for my children and my wife, the first people I meet in an ordinary day, or for any of the other people I meet during the day, is to hold them in my Space and honor them. Honoring to me is the first step in loving and sometimes is more important than loving. Honoring is a form of holding to my mind. I hold them without expectation and without projection. This does not mean I don't have memory of them. I've known Julie for thirty-five years and have thirty-five years of absolutely wonderful memories. We have a history together. But whenever I see Julie or engage with her, my Incarnational Spirituality training tells me that I am meeting her for the first time that her Space is infinite and I can never therefore know it completely. What I don't know about Julie is always infinitely larger than what I do. Therefore, I try to meet her and my kids with a dual mind. The Cup part of the mind contains all the memories of our histories together. It gives particularity and specificity to our relationships. But the Space part of my mind is ever new, for no matter how much Space holds, it can always hold more. Space is the Intelligence of possibility and emergence. It is what is not yet known, while the Cup holds what is known: the specificity of biography.

We are constantly engaging, holding, and transmitting to and with each other various kinds of energies on various levels, from physical sensations, pheromones, electromagnetic feelings, and visual clues to etheric energies, astral thoughts and feelings, spiritual impulses and so on. The impulse of Cups is to broadcast "Cupping" energy. There can be a tendency for our Cup to shape other Cups to be like us. We want people to behave according to our expectations, to fulfill our thoughts and desires, to meet our needs, to be controllable and predictable, all of which are Cup characteristics. These characteristics are perfectly appropriate in some circumstances but not in all. Problems in relationship occur all the time when our Cup-intelligences (Please remember that I'm using this metaphorically) try to shape other cups to look like us, to contain what we contain, to not be bigger (Cup-envy, you know!), and so on. And our Space-intelligences can betray us when they want us all to be just, well, Spacey, beyond particulars, beyond selves, beyond structure and form. But when my Cup can use its "Cupness" or "Cup-energy" to support your Cup and help it be a better

Cup for you, then I am being an Agent of Incarnation. And when my Space can support your Space in a similar way and help it be a better Space for you, then I am also being an Agent of Incarnation.

I am open and alert to ways of doing this. This is not a specific technique. It is profoundly situational. It is an attitude and an attunement. It is an act of seeing and an act of listening to another. It can involve such practical techniques as non-violent communication, tone of voice, paying attention, honoring the person in front of us, also listening to our own felt senses of what is transpiring, and maintaining boundaries—theirs and ours. Anything I can learn that helps me with communication, recognizing and honoring my feelings and thoughts and those of another, being gracious and spacious, being comfortable, setting appropriate boundaries, and being comfortable with being myself and comfortable with the other being different from me, is a tool of Incarnational Spirituality. The ways we can help another's incarnation are numerous. Many of them are purely energetic, purely active on levels of thought and feeling, while others are physical actions.

In our Starshaman Training and other long-term programs and classes, time is spent just on learning how to be in one's own sovereignty and incarnational power and then how to support another in theirs. So I can't give you a blow-by-blow of "I said this," or "I did this." Indeed to do so overly concretizes what Incarnational Spirituality is and turns it into a series of techniques, which is not the whole picture. So let's just say that in every encounter, I monitor my energy, my thoughts and feelings, and I look at how I can engage with the situation and with others in a manner that enhances all our capacities to incarnate. These would be the capacities to be, to have boundaries, to connect, to engage, and to emerge and grow.

In my own case, I take time several times during the day to reflect on how this process is going for me. This is not judging how I'm succeeding or not at Incarnational Spirituality or in engaging with my world; It is just an act of witnessing in order to understand and hold what I am doing, how I am being, and what might need change. I am also witnessing what could emerge: how I might do it better or more effectively or more authentically. Such moments of reflection, which can hardly be called meditations, are common to many spiritual practices, for self-reflection is a fundamental capacity and art that is truly vital to spiritual growth. There is nothing new here except perhaps the context of incarnation and the particular cosmology within which I work which influences just how I reflect and what I'm particularly looking for.

I would like to now preview the concept of the Incarnational Field that I'll be working with next. Each of us has one such a field. I'll define it properly later in the text. Suffice it to say that one lens through which to see our incarnations is through our relationships, connections, and creative expressions. Let me imagine that you are an author and that you write books and use that imagining as an example. From an Incarnational Spirituality point of view, each book you write is part of your incarnation, part of your Cup and Space. Anytime anyone engages with one of your books, they are engaging with you. This means that one way you could practice Incarnational Spirituality is to be aware of this and to hold the original manuscript of your book, the one that gets printed, and see it as an agent of blessing sent forth by the you, the author. Though you probably haven't thought of it in this way, from an Incarnational Spirituality perspective, I might say that each book potentially has the capacity and the intention to enable whoever reads it to incarnate more fully and be more capable. This even includes connecting and engaging with a particular software program and what can potentially emerge from that engagement. You could see each book as an angel, a messenger, of your sacred intent to serve, help and empower others as a particular expression of sacredness. Believe me, holding a book in this way in your own mind and heart and releasing it into the world, honoring its livingness and seeing it as an extension of your Cup and Space, as your incarnation seeking to aid the incarnation of others will have an effect. If you bless your book, it becomes a blessing for all who use it. This is an example of a very practical expression of Incarnational Spirituality.

What I have been writing about up to now has been in service to the first level of change, which is within yourself and in your perspective of who you are in yourself and in the world. The distinctive element of Incarnational Spirituality is for me the felt sense of being a Source. This Sourceness is who I am as an individuated, personal, physical personality as well as my soul, my higher self or my spirit (or any other image of transpersonal-ness). I am <u>not</u> spirit having a human experience.

I am "what I am" having a human spiritual experience or a spiritual human experience What "I am" is as much an incarnate self as it is a numinous one. I don't descend into the earth or into a body; that to me is not what incarnation is. My movement into this physical plane from non-physical planes is the process of embodiment, <u>not</u> the process of incarnation, or at least not all of it. Incarnation is what I am and what I do whatever "plane" or realm or domain my outermost expression happens to be on, and part of that "doing" of Incarnation is being a Source. Being a Source of what? Many things, but what is most significant and important here is being a source of sacredness. I do not pass through sacredness from a higher level to this one. I <u>generate</u> it. We are all generating sacredness as an activity and a presence in ways that are commensurate with and appropriate to our capacities, our environments, our Cup-ness, and our Spaciousness.

My metaphor for this is the way stars generate the stuff, the substance, in the form of heavy atoms, from which the rest of the cosmos is made. In a metaphoric way, we, as spiritual stars, through the process of incarnation (which is like the process of atomic fusion within a star), generate. We generate life stuff, soul stuff, personhood stuff, world stuff, love stuff, compassion stuff, forgiveness stuff, insight stuff, enlightenment stuff, fun stuff, laughter stuff, challenging stuff, all of which is sacred stuff. So when I go through my day, I do so as a star, being mindful of what I am radiating, what I am generating, what kind of stuff I'm putting out, and what kind of stuff I'm participating in, along with all that comes from the other "stars" around me. That is the Incarnational Spirituality perspective, at least, as I understand it currently. Hope that's clear! And exciting! And down-to-earth!

the third exercise, **Standing**, which follows illustrates and embodies the principles about which I have been speaking.

Notes and Reflections

Exercise Three: Standing

This is the core exercise in the practice of Incarnational Spirituality. I have adapted it somewhat in my years of teaching, but basically it is the same as when I first started assigning it to students. This exercise has physical, mental, emotional, and spiritual aspects to it. These aspects are designed to be done all at once, but I'll present them as separate categories.

Physical:

The physical action of this exercise is simple. From a sitting position, you simply stand up. Be aware of the physical sensation and felt sense of standing. Feel the work of your body, the power of balance that keeps you upright. If you are already standing, become aware that you are standing and be mindful of the felt sense of standing. If you are physically unable to stand, you can still assume an inner attitude of standing, perhaps simply by straightening your spine as much as possible.

Emotional:

Feel the power of being upright. Feel the strength of rising up against the gravity of the earth. Feel how standing singles you out and expresses your individuality. You stand for what you believe you stand up to be counted. Standing proclaims that you are here. Feel the strength and presence of your identity and sovereignty.

Mental:

Celebrate your humanness. You are an upright being. You emerge from the mass of nature, from the vegetative and animal states into a realm of thinking and imagining. In standing, you hands are released from providing locomotion. Feel the freedom of your hands that don't have to support you but can now be used to create, manipulate, touch, and express your thoughts and imagination.

Magical:

When you stand, your spine becomes a magical staff, the *axis mundi* (center) of your personal world, generating the field that embraces you. The spine is the traditional wizard's staff along which dragon power flows and the centers of energy sing in resonance with the cosmos.

Spiritual:

Standing, you are the incarnate link between heaven and earth. Your energy rises into the sky and descends into the earth. Light descends and ascends, swirling along your spine in a marriage of matter and spirit. This energy is both personal and the transpersonal, giving birth to something new, something human, individual and unique. In doing this exercise of Standing, you stand. As you do so, work through these levels of sensation, feeling, thought, energy, and spirit, appreciating the power, the freedom, the sovereignty, and the presence emerging from the simple act of standing. When you have finished doing it, record your experiences in your journal. Do this recording each time you do this exercise, so you can see what emerges for you over a period of time.

Notes and Reflections

Chapter Three
Terms and **Definitions**

This is where we begin to sort out some of the different terms found in the premises in the previous chapter. Here I want to describe sovereignty, boundaries, personality and source definitions in some detail. There are cosmological assumptions behind these definitions that I'm not going to get into in this text. I ask you to treat them as hypotheses. I basically want you to appreciate what I mean by

Sovereignty and its importance in the overall framework of Incarnational Spirituality.

Sovereignty

Sovereignty, as shown graphically in the picture, is the "line of sacredness and being" that is our link with the Generative Mystery. It is the essence, sum or presence of our sacredness, Identity, Self, Individuality, and Soul as manifested in our physical incarnation. I use the word Sovereignty because I want to suggest the idea of "self-rule" or "self-governing." When we speak of the conditioned personality, the part of us that we take on from the world and that is shaped by the world, in a way, this is the part of us that is "other-ruled" or "other-governed." Sovereignty, by contrast, is the capacity and function within us that enables us to express our unique "isness" or being, our will and "I"- ness. It is the power that enables us to govern our selves. I also use Sovereignty in the mythic sense that was once associated with Kingship. The King was sovereign but this Sovereignty was granted by the Land and involved a responsibility to care for the Land. In other words, Sovereignty is not a unilateral, private power; the capacity to do anything one wants. It is a gift bestowed from the "Commons," from the Whole of Life. The function of Sovereignty is to enable me to govern myself so my unique contribution to life is preserved and not covered over by "outer conditioning." I can contribute and participate in the unique ways I have to the wellbeing of others and the world as a whole. Sovereignty, is not the same as selfishness, self-orientation or being personality-centered in any limited or constrained way. It is a power that links us with our own sacredness and with the sacredness in the world.

The main reason for going through all the cosmological definitions and relationships above is to provide a context for understanding what I mean by Sovereignty. It is the expression of our individual sacredness, the "will-to-be" within us. It is also like an axis or thread around which all other manifestations of self and identity are arranged. But in an interesting way, it is less personal than our individuality, our "I". It is a function or an activity through which the "I" manifests. The Standing and Self-Light exercises are both ways of attuning to one's own

Sovereignty. In standing, I am emulating the axis-like aspect of this condition or activity. In the Self-Light exercise (page 60), I am attuning to the presence and quality, the Light, of this condition. I have picked the word "sovereignty" because of its two associations: one with self-governance and the integrity of the individual and the other the mythic sense of "care for the land," or care for the whole. In other words, sovereignty confers power but it's a power that is a gift from a larger wholeness and ultimately needs to be used in service or contribution to that larger wholeness.

Sovereignty describes a relationship between the sacred and us. If it were not for the sacred, and for all other beings that form the whole vast realm of the Other, we would not have the experience or gift of Self, Individuality, and Personhood. Yet, there are experiences, powers, and capacities that can only be experienced by a Self or within the context of individuality and selfness. That is something we contribute. A problem can arise in how we think about or envision Ultimacy as God or the Sacred or the Generative Mystery. More often than not, we associate such a state with qualities like Unity, Oneness, (No-Self), and the One, and not with Separation, Distinctness, Difference, or the Many.

The sacred is often imaged as an "ocean" while the individual is a "drop" whose destiny is to return to or merge with the ocean. A drop, though, can do things that an ocean cannot. An ocean, for example, cannot become a teardrop shape. If one says that individual seek the Unity the way drops seek the ocean, it could equally be said that through evaporation, the ocean seeks to become drops and the Unity seeks to become individual. Which is the true destination or destiny? One could imagine a Monty Python type rendition of this, ala "Life of Brian," in which one faction seeks to follow the drop while the other seeks to follow the ocean! In my own experience, neither "drop" nor "ocean" fully capture the Mystery of the sacred, nor for that matter the Mystery of Self. Mystery is accessible from both the "drop" state and the "ocean" state. This is the perspective of Incarnational Spirituality. One is not choosing between the drop or the ocean, the self or the no-self, the particle or the wave, the personal or the transpersonal. Each needs to be honored and seen in paradoxical partnership in order to attune to what is neither drop nor ocean, but rather the Mystery behind both. In doing this, one strategy is to reclaim the spirituality, the radiance, the value, and the power of the drop, the individual and the personal.

Sovereignty, as I use it, represents a middle ground, so between the drop and the ocean, the individual and the Wholeness, the one and the Oneness. When I speak of "standing in one's Sovereignty," I mean going to a place of inner strength and integrity where one can attune to and experience one's empersonal spirit, one's Self-Light, and one's sacredness. This is not quite the same felt sense as going to the "God within." I admit to having trouble with that phrase. The image this conjures up for me is that of a spark of Light that rides around inside my body and my mind. To me, however, sacredness does not ride around within us as some separate entity but rather it *is* we. Our bodies and minds are part of the sacred. I tend to think of the sacred more as an activity than a thing. The well known "God is a Verb" image first suggested by Buckminster Fuller comes to mind. I think of standing in Sovereignty as standing more mindfully in the activity of sacredness, such as openness, holding, love, compassion, etc. As I implied above, standing in Sovereignty also implies a way of standing in relationship. And that brings up the issue of boundaries.

Boundaries

As implied in the material I've written earlier, an important part of the creative process is the establishment of differentiation. Differentiation is an engine that powers the flow and interaction of energies. A metaphor for this is weather, in which wind is generated by differences between temperature and pressure within different regions.

Differentiation implies boundary conditions. Such boundaries can be hard (like a brick wall) or soft (like the boundary between space and the earth's atmosphere, which is not a sudden change but a gradual decrease (or increase, depending on the direction you're moving!) in the number of gaseous molecules floating about. When I lived in Phoenix, Arizona, back in the early Sixties, some of the shopping malls were experimenting with "air curtain" entryways. This was a blast or curtain of air that you walked through, a very permeable membrane indeed and invisible for the most part, but it kept the air-conditioned air inside and the hot desert air outside.

We create all kinds of boundaries around ourselves. Our skin is one very obvious physical boundary. Our attitudes and beliefs can be another that is less obvious. There are energetic boundaries as well belonging to what the esoteric traditions call our "subtle bodies." A boundary can be passive and simply act to protect us or to receive and absorb the impacts of life. It can also be active, a tool of engagement. Metaphorically, I can use my hands to push people away or to draw them in. Incarnational Spirituality honors boundaries of all kinds; there would be no incarnation without them. There would be no relationships, for relationships only take place where two or more things are differentiated from each other in some manner (i.e. possess a boundary). A boundary is a limit but it is not necessarily a constriction. One can have boundaries and still be open and engaging. A boundary is simply a mode of engagement, not the walls of a prison. Many years ago John, my non-physical friend and mentor, said to me, "In the future, there will be a spirituality of boundaries. Spirituality will focus on what happens at boundaries." What does happen at boundaries? Information is exchanged in various forms; differences come together. There can be conflict and there can be co-creativity. Something new can emerge. The sacred can arise or be suppressed by what happens between us. We can be enlarged or diminished by what occurs across our boundaries in our encounter with others. In our classes, we explore a number of different kinds of boundaries and what can happen at them.

Boundaries give another meaning to Sovereignty. Sovereignty is the capacity to live mindfully and safely at one's boundaries. If I see Sovereignty as a capacity and power of self-governance and free will, then my boundaries represent the volume within which this Sovereignty operates. Boundaries define, express, configure, and protect our Sovereignty. If my Sovereignty is diminished, it is because in some manner my boundaries have been breached or diminished as well, and vice versa. If I have boundary problems in my life, I have Sovereignty problems as well. The two go hand in hand. But equally, the communal nature of Sovereignty means that it is a capacity that seeks to protect, uphold, and preserve the integrity of boundaries in others, since that is the way to uphold their Sovereignty and the integrity and power of their incarnational process.

One very simple expression of this is to be dedicated to preserving and honoring the dignity of everyone whom we meet. To damage or take away another's dignity (and it can happen in so many subtle ways) is to risk damaging their boundaries and their Sovereignty. This is one reason I speak more of honoring than of love. True love always includes honor and the respect of another's dignity and integrity, but we don't always think of it that way. Further, love can be an excuse for trampling across another's boundaries and dignity by assuming rights and privileges that are not necessarily there. We assume that if there's love, we can get away with more than if love isn't there; after all, isn't love never needing to say you're sorry? Ha!. So I talk about honoring quite explicitly so that it is not subsumed and overlooked in any sappy definition of "loving."

Personality

One element I did not define above but which is shown in the next picture is the personality.

There are all kinds of definitions, thoughts, images, insights, and descriptions concerning the personality and what it is. It is obviously a complex topic. Within Incarnational Spirituality, we define the personality broadly as the "particularizing function <u>and</u> the boundary of engagement with the world." Incarnational Spirituality does not see the personality as an obstruction standing between us and the sacred or us and enlightenment. Not that there are not aspects or expressions of the personality that can do that, but that is not a definition of the personality as a whole. I see the personality not so much as a thing but as an activity, a function that replicates the Cup and Space relationship we talked about earlier. Most people probably think of their personalities as themselves. It's the sum of all their feelings and thoughts, patterns of behavior, memories, sense of self, and so on. Certainly it is all these things, or at least it holds the content that makes up all these things. In this sense, the personality is the Cup and Space of our physical identity and is often differentiated from our Soul or our spiritual Self, sometimes to the detriment of the personality.

We can also see personality as a function, a magical ally, that enables the comparative vastness of the soul to become one with and engage with a more constricted realm of bounded entities. Through the function of the personality, the wave becomes the particle, so to speak.

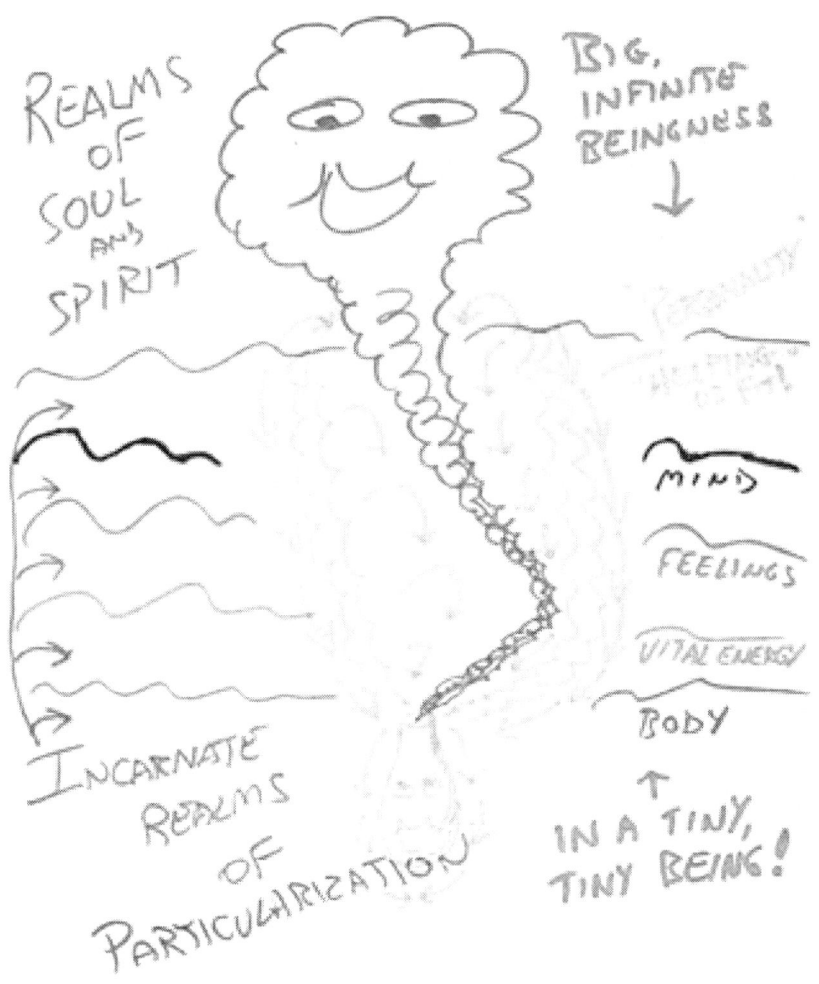

From my inner point of view, the personality is what enables the multi-dimensionality of the Soul to manifest within the four-dimensionality (three dimensions of space, one dimension of time) of the planetary incarnational realm. We experience the multi-dimensionality of the inner worlds when we dream and time and space seem so different, so nonlinear and "quantum-like", from everyday life. By the incarnate realm I mean the domains of the psyche (concrete, object oriented mind and emotion), chi or vital energy, and physical matter. It is the confluence of thought, feeling, life energy, and physical body. This is the realm in which the personality functions. Part of that functioning is to provide means for the Soul to engage with and be part of this realm. The usual image for this relationship is often one of occupant and vehicle, like a car and driver. One might also picture the personality as a kind of "space suit" that allows the Soul to function in a realm that otherwise would be barred to it.

In some of my classes and in this picture I have represented the personality as the force that enables the genie of the soul to inhabit a bottle. It allows for a Big, Vast Beingness to manifest as a Tiny, Tiny Being. (I take this image from Disney's animated movie, Aladdin, in which Robin Williams as the genie bemoans having to be a Cosmic Being of Infinite Power bound into a little, tiny bottle.) As such it is more than a Cup, it is also a Cup-Maker. The personality is a soul-function that enables us to "fit" in this world. Please note that the bottle is not the personality, at least not entirely. The whole energy field that moves the genie into the bottle is the personality, which includes the bottle as one of its outer expressions. However, this image is not quite dynamic and holistic enough to actually capture the relationship as I see and experience it on the inner. Instead, think of paying attention to something in particular.

What is the inner mechanism of Will that allows you to focus on one thing in particular and give it your full attention? Imagine that you are the world's smartest physicist and you are explaining what physics is about to an average kindergarten student. There is so much that you know, understand, and can do that the six-year old would not understand and could not do. To engage successfully with this young person, you have to pay attention to him or her and filter the vastness and complexity of your concepts and understanding into images and terms that make sense to a six-year old. What is the mechanism of mind, attention, imagination, feeling, empathy, connection, and engagement that allows you to do that? Whatever that is for you, that is what the personality is in relationship to the soul, a means of focusing attention, connection, and engagement from one realm and state of being to another that is comparatively more particulate and less complex. That is why I think of the personality as an activity, a function, a mechanism, more than a thing that is separate from the soul, like a vehicle the soul rides around in. The personality is a complex subject. It can be viewed through lenses of psychology, cognitive biology, anatomy and physiology, social studies, religion and spirituality, magic and esotericism. Each lens will give you a different perspective and emphasize different elements. To say that the personality is an activity or function enabling us to pay attention to and engage a particulate world is only another lens. It is not intended to be an alternative description or definition to those offered by the other lenses. I certainly do not claim it is the "true" definition, more accurate than the others are because it comes from supersensory perception and cognition.

It is a definition with a purpose. The purpose is to open for you an experience of yourself, your personal self, that is not antagonistic to or separate from your spiritual, transpersonal selves or Soul. Its purpose is to help you experience that your personality, your everyday self, your incarnate personhood, is a spiritual manifestation that is quite capable of radiance. It is also capable of being a source of spiritual energy not in spite of what it is but because of what it is as part of the act of incarnation. This is not the whole picture either. The perception that the personality is a function of the soul (from which arises the construct we usually think of as "personality") does not also say that it is a perfect function or one that proceeds without error. There are reasons why the personality can be seen and has been seen as an obstruction to our spiritual capacities. Incarnation is not a perfected process by any means. I will not go into the negative or obstructive sides of the personality here, or why they exist. That aspect is part of the overall teaching of an Incarnational Spirituality, but it requires more time and depth than we have here. I do wish to make a point, though. When we understand the spiritual roots and activity of the personality and come to see it as part of our wholeness, then we discover within us quite powerful capacities for dealing with the errors, the negativity, and woundedness that can become the experience of personality for so many of us.

A final word about the incarnate realm. In many esoteric and metaphysical traditions, this realm is seen as divided into layers or different subsidiary realms. Usually this division is presented hierarchically and takes a form roughly as I've presented it in the picture. There are the levels of Body, Etheric or Vital Energy, Feelings, Concrete Mind, and Abstract Mind. Sometimes the feelings and concrete mind are seen as one blended manifestation and are called together the "astral" plane. Though traditional language usually discusses these layers or levels as actual dimensions (they do represent different frequencies and manifestations of energy, rather like the different colored layers of Jell-O in some deserts), they may also be seen as functions or orientations within a holism. Rather than thinking of the personality as split between these different layers, perhaps with one layer nested within another, we can think of the personality in a different way. It can be a personality (or the incarnate personal consciousness) that acts a single coherent presence that can manifest many functions; an energetic function, a thinking/feeling function, a function of imagination, and a function of abstract thought. If I do, then I can more readily think of myself as an "individuality" or "I" expressing physically, emotionally, mentally or energetically as a wholeness. It is a "holism" that is more than just physical, mental, emotional, spiritual, As you can see, I'm all for any perspective that helps us experience our integrity, coherency, and wholeness as well as our separate parts!

Source

The final idea I want to present to complete our definitions is that of being a source. There are many ways that we are sources. We are sources of thoughts, feelings, behaviors, and physical substances. More specifically, we are sources of spiritual radiance. Through our Self-Light, we can contribute spiritual power and blessing to our world. Now we can certainly, through attunement and alignment, act as participants in passing through spiritual power from higher levels of life, (i.e. from the spiritual realms). We often do so through prayer and meditation. The idea of being a source is more immediate. It affirms that we can be more than just a tube through which Light and spirit pass into the world, more than just a recipient, more than just a consumer can. It affirms that such Light and spirit can also originate with us in unique and effective ways. Certainly this is true when we perform acts of compassion, kindness, and caring. It is also true at a more fundamental level. Being what we are, as manifestations of Soul and Sacredness, there is never a time when we are not radiating. That radiation can be obscured, covered up, diluted and distorted with "noise" and static, but it is always Present nonetheless. Spiritual growth is often not so much a process of gaining something new as it is of uncovering the treasure that was buried in our backyard all the time.

As part of an Incarnational Spirituality, the idea of being a source goes further. Imagine a star as a metaphor. Within the heat and pressure at the heart of a star, nuclear processes are engaged that result in atomic fusion and the production of new, heavier atoms. This process is what generates the radiance, light and heat of a star. It is also what generates the heavy atoms, such as iron and carbon that become the building blocks of the cosmos. Without the atomic material born in the womb of stars, there would be no planets, no life, and no universe, as we know it. There is a similar process that occurs in us. If I look deeply at the energetic processes occurring in our non-physical, subtle bodies or aspects of being, I can see exchanges and transformations going on in all of us daily that generate "life stuff" ("mind stuff," "feeling stuff," "spiritual stuff"). These exchanges, like the heavy atoms, become substances from which we all are constantly building our individual and collective worlds. We generate ideas and feelings that motivate or inform others, just as we are informed and motivated by the thoughts and emotions of others. More importantly, energy is generated as a form of radiance and Light.

We are most familiar and aware of this process through our self-reflection and interior work on the psychological, psychic, and spiritual materials within us. Let's say I feel an anger rising in me that would lead me to strike out at another. If instead I seize the energy of that anger and transform it into something less hurtful, like a willingness to listen and understand another, or a determination to bring justice into a situation in non-violent ways, I am performing an act of energetic transformation that generates Light. I am turning one kind of energy into another. An important part of any spiritual practice is the work we do within ourselves to transform experiences into wisdom, to assimilate new knowledge, to turn negative feelings into positive ones, and to transform self-defeating images into ones that motivate and empower. This sounds like good psychological and spiritual work. It is also energetic alchemy. It effects a transformation of one kind of energy into another, one kind of "subtle atom" into another. In that transformation, quite apart from any good results that may accrue, such as deeper understanding or greater lovingness, it generates Light. We really are living stars.

Another aspect of being a source is that it can create a powerful shift in attitude. So often in our world we are seen as recipients, planets reflecting the light of others, consumers, conduits for something to pass through from one place or condition to another. When I begin to think of myself as a unique source, then I define myself with images such as producer, contributor, and valuable participant in society. I can begin to see in myself a power to bless, to nurture, to comfort, to uplift, to love: all the qualities and capacities we associate with spirit. I become a radiance in my life, not just a sponge! The idea of being a source is an empowering one, and it also suggests the power and responsibility that comes through our participation in life. We are constantly radiating and generating, but we are not the only ones doing so. Everything does so. We are like stars in a galaxy of radiant sources. Stars are everywhere we look, some brighter, some less bright, but all of them generating the stuff from which the cosmos is constructed. We, too, generate "stuff" from which our human and planetary world molds and shapes and constitutes itself.

Some time ago I attended the birthday of the eldest daughter of two friends of mine. Knowing it was her 34th birthday was itself a sobering and joyful thought, showing as it did both how time has passed and celebrating a friendship that has lasted over half my life. One of her friends gave her a new book, just published this month, called <u>Social Intelligence</u> by Daniel Goleman, who also wrote <u>Emotional Intelligence</u>. Not having seen the book before, I glanced through it and read the flyleaf on the cover, discovering that the author was exploring some of the very same concepts of "sourceness" and participation that I'm covering briefly here. Here are a couple quotes from the flyleaf:

"Far more than we are consciously aware, our daily encounters with parents, spouses, bosses, and even strangers shape our brains and affect cells throughout our bodies—down to the level of our genes—for good or ill."

"Our reactions to others, and theirs to us, have a far-reaching biological impact, sending out cascades of hormones that regulate everything from our hearts to our immune systems, making good relationships act like vitamins—and bad relationships like poisons. We can "catch" other people's emotions the way we catch a cold, and the consequences of isolation or relentless social stress can be life-shortening."

Of course, Goleman is exploring the outer, social dimensions of how we participate, affect, and shape our world, but he is doing so at a more basic level than most of us think about. I am suggesting that in Incarnational Spirituality this participation and affect goes even deeper. Where Goleman speaks of us being "constantly engaged in a 'neural ballet' that connects us brain to brain with those around us." I suggest that we are also involved in an energetic ballet of subtle energies that also connect us and shape us in profound ways that make us "co-incarnates" with each other. This ballet is influenced and informed by our capacities as sources and not just as recipients.

Notes and Reflections

Exercise Four:
Self-Light

The purpose of this exercise is to honor yourself and to invoke the spiritual energy of your incarnate personhood. We need to be able to tap the spiritual roots of our everyday self, roots that are deeply connected with all of life, with the earth, with the sun and stars, with the cosmos, and with the sacred. We need to connect with ourselves as a spiritual source, a source of blessing and spiritual energy. We need to do this not just as a receiver or consumer of "spiritual goods." In nature-based and land-based spiritual traditions, there is acknowledgment of the "Light within the Earth." In Incarnational Spirituality, I would similarly acknowledge the Light within the self. We need to discover and acknowledge this earthly, personal Light. It is an act of self-oriented mysticism. That is the object of this exercise.

Preparation

You can do this exercise entirely in your imagination. Just do the dedications inwardly imagining, if you wish, the lighting of the candles. If you want to do this exercise physically, then preparation is simple. Just arrange a space that you can dedicate to this exercise and in which you feel focused, safe, comfortable, and honored. It is a magical and sacred space you are creating. You can arrange this space however you wish. Minimally, there should be two candles and at least one item that is "talismanic" for you. This item can be a reminder or touchstone of something important, vital, wonderful, uplifting, or honoring about your personal self. For example, I might use a small stone that I took from a river where I often played as a young teenager, the scene of many happy memories. I might also use a stone from the land around the Findhorn Community in Scotland where I lived and worked in the early Seventies. It doesn't matter what the item is so long as you have something that enables you to appreciate your everyday self. A mundane object may work better than one with religious or spiritual significance or affinity, as you want to tune in to your personal rather than your transpersonal self.

The Dedication

Sit down and light one of the candles. As you do so, dedicate this space and all that you do within it to the sacred and to the highest good for all beings. While you do not wish to focus upon transpersonal or transcendent realities in this exercise, the sacred is present to all levels and all forms of existence. The honoring of yourself is an honoring of the sacred from which you emerge. Light the second candle from the first one and dedicate this space to the Light that emerges from your incarnational self, the Light of being a physical, personal being. This Light is unique. It is not simply a transmission or emanation from a higher level projected into this one. It comes into being as you incarnate and is a spiritual presence unique to you, unique to this realm of being, and at the same time one with all Light everywhere on all levels throughout the inner and outer cosmos.

The Exercise - Part One

Sit and appreciate yourself. Look at the candles and think into what they mean. What is the Light within incarnation, the Light to which incarnation gives birth and expression? What is the Light within your earthly self? Look at any icons or talismans you may have in the space with you. Let them remind you of the wonder of your life, the beauty of being alive and being yourself, the accomplishments you have made, the people who love you, the people you love, the dreams and visions you have, and the creative things you do or enjoy. Be with yourself as you would be with a comfortable and loved old friend. In this exercise, you are seeking to enter the felt sense in your body, heart, and mind of your goodness and rightness, of the pleasure and honor of being you, of the unique gift that you are to creation, of the unique service and contribution only you can render. You are entering the presence of your self, the way a child might enter Disneyland, with excitement and wonder, with joy and a sense of play. What about those parts of you that are not nice, that create problems, that feel wounded and suffering, that are in pain or remorse? You certainly should acknowledge them. In this exercise, you are not saying you are all goodness and light. You do not deny the unintegrated and negative aspects of your life. Indeed, you see this material as compost from which wisdom can arise. It is part of you and you want to embrace it as well. But in this exercise, you are concentrating on the overall rightness and power of being an incarnate being. You are celebrating the spirit of being an individual. Again, you are not analyzing yourself or trying to heal yourself in anyway. That is a different emphasis, perfectly correct in its own place, but this is not that place.

Part Two

You are going to journey inward in imagination to the Light within your Self. How you do this is up to you. It is important that you craft this journey yourself since it needs to express your uniqueness. In its barest essentials, it is turning your attention to Light, the holy flame that burns in the foundation hearth of your existence as a person. As in the mystical tradition, you are seeking union with your own Light, the Light of your earthly self, the Light within your human identity. You can certainly skip any kind of imaginal journeying and just go to this Light. Indeed, the object of this exercise is to recognize the feel and presence of this Light within you so you may go to it at any time of the day no matter what you are doing. However it may be helpful, at least in the beginning, as a way of engaging heart and mind in the process, to formulate a journey into this Light. It is best if you create your own path, using images and symbols meaningful to you. You could walk beside a river, journey into an ancient temple, climb a mountain, walk through fertile farmland, whatever is meaningful to you and gives you a sense of moving from one state of consciousness to another.

At the end of whatever journeys you create for yourself, come to a place where your Incarnational Light, your Self-Light, is present, evident, and accessible. You want to step into that Light of your earthly self and feel it presence and radiant power within you, as you, in a way you can draw upon. You might imagine, for example, that this Self-Light appears as a pillar of Light just taller than you are. You can feel it inviting you to step into it. You step into it and this Light embraces you. You are surrounded by it, held by it, filled by it. You are this Light. Take however long you need to enjoy and absorb this experience. Pay attention to the felt sense of being in and of this Light. When you feel complete with this (which might manifest as a sense of restlessness or of wishing to move on), see that this Self-Light is part of a vaster Light. It is part of the Light of your soul, the Light of your spirit, the Light within the Earth, the Light within the Cosmos. It is one with the Light of the sacred, and it resonates with all Lights and all Light everywhere. Enjoy this communion of Light that honors Self-Light but expands beyond it as well. Then, standing in this Light, remember and picture in your mind your physical body sitting in the space you have created. With grace and deliberation, step from imaginal place, carrying the felt sense of this Self-Light and the blessing of All Light, back into your body, back into the space around you. Open your eyes. The journey is complete. The exercise is finished.

Ending

When you restore your attention to your everyday world, the first thing you do is to physically touch something in the spirit and felt sense of the Light you have experienced. You ground that Light through an immediate act of relationship and of sharing it with something in your world. This simple act brings you back into your everyday world but also is an act of blessing, an expression of what your Self-Light is all about.

When you have finished, record your experiences on the following pages or in your journal. Do this recording each time you do this exercise, so you can see what emerges for you over a period of time.

Notes and Reflections

Exercise Five:
Blessing or "Sourcing"

In the previous exercise, the intent is to come to a felt sense of your Self-Light, some inner familiarity and awareness that allows you to go to that inner place and Light when you think of it, without having to necessarily go through the whole exercise itself. In this follow-up exercise, this is what you do to begin with. This is a very simple (and probably quite familiar) exercise that can be done in as short a time as a matter of seconds or as long a time as you wish and as is comfortable for you before you get restless and wish you were doing something else!

1. Begin by entering your Self-Light

2. Take a moment to appreciate this radiant source within you, the generative spiritual emanation of your own unique incarnation and individuality.

3. Imagine and feel this Light radiating out from you into your body, filling all your cells with its power and blessing (and gratefulness). Feel it radiating out from you to your immediate surroundings. Feel it radiating out from you to family and friends. Feel it radiating out from you into the larger world of nature and humanity. Feel it radiating out from you to embrace the day that is about to unfold, the time that is not yet but which will bring you this day experiences, contacts, and connections old and new, familiar and unknown, expected and unexpected.

4. Give thanks for this Self-Light. If you wish, you can now open to any transpersonal or non-personal sources of Light that are meaningful. Receive its blessing, attuning to it, feeling its resonance with your own Self-Light, and then participating in radiating this greater, collective Light and blessing out into your world in a similar way to step 3.

5. Give thanks for these blessings, and step forth into your day.

6. When you have finished doing this exercise, record your experiences in your journal. Do this recording each time you do this exercise, so you can see what emerges for you over a period of time. Or spend some time in the evening to reflect back and record your experiences during the day from this place of sourcing.

A friend of mine who is a wonderful college teacher of things spiritual, shamanic, esoteric, religious, and philosophical once remarked to me that he thought we were like the old gaslights that used to hang on walls before electricity was used. We burned with an inner flame that radiated light through the glass of our individuality, he said, like the old glass-lights, the interior surface of the glass could collect soot and become dirty, diminishing our light. From time to time we needed to clean the soot off!

Exercise Six:
Alternative Sourcing Exercise

See yourself and your Self-Light within a glass sphere. Around all the interior surface of this sphere are representations of family, friends, people you know or have known, your work, the place you live, nature, humanity, your expectations for the day ahead, and so on. Imagine as many or as few images as you wish or are able. You might just imagine one or two and be aware in the back of your mind that other images are there too. This is not a mental exercise in listing and creating images but a felt sense of working with the connections that are important to you. As you see them, these images are not as transparent as they might be. They are covered with the soot of your expectations, memories, preconceptions, opinions, judgments, familiarity, definitions, and the like. Stand in your Self-Light and feel and see this Light increase, playing over the interior surface of this glass sphere and illuminating all these images and representations, symbols and pictures. Let this Light carry love to all these images. See your Light and lovingness brightening them, burning away the soot, burning through all the stuff that may have accumulated around or upon each image so that the image itself becomes clean, clear, and transparent, allowing your Light to shine through to the world. Hold all that these images represent to you in your Light and lovingness, giving thanks for the many ways they connect you to the world and enable you to engage, participate, and incarnate, thereby fulfilling the deep will-to-be of your Soul. As they become clear, you are dropping away accumulated thoughts, feelings, judgments, opinions, and the like that may disconnect you from the people, places, and things represented by these images or that cause you to project shadows of expectation upon them or into your world. You are liberating yourself and those whose images you are illuminating from the "soot" of the familiar and the past, and allowing yourself to see all about you with fresh, transparent, and grateful mind. If you wish, you can repeat this exercise as above by drawing in and upon transpersonal and non-personal sources of Light to clean the inside of your sphere, the inside of your consciousness. This way your Light can radiate cleanly, clearly, and purely into the world. Again, record your experience.

Practice A

A word about practice: well, two words really. First, practice makes perfect. These exercises pay dividends to you if you do them more than once. Second, you can link these exercises, or ones like them that you devise, into a sequence. So, with just what we've covered so far, you could begin your day with a moment of Standing, gaining a felt sense of all that means for you. Then you can let that felt sense lead you into attuning and standing in your Self- Light, appreciating all that means to you and feeling how that lives in your body and in your heart and mind. Next you can turn that Self-Light outwards to bless your world (perhaps cleaning some soot away in the process), and end by joining in partnership with other sources of Light as you go forth to enter your day. The other exercises we'll be learning can be added to this sequence so that by the end there will be a simple process you can use if you wish that will embody some of the most important elements of Incarnational Spirituality.

Notes and Reflections

Chapter Four
Holding and Blessing

Among other things, Incarnational Spirituality is a practice to develop certain skills and capacities. We've already explored two of them: standing in Sovereignty (which includes the skill of maintaining and using one's boundaries as tools of connection and engagement) and attuning to one's Self-Light and identity as a generative source. Practicing these skills can certainly stimulate changes in one's self-image and how a person carries himself or herself in the world. Two other important skills are Holding and Blessing. The skills we have already looked at mainly focus on an individual's own personal interior life. Holding and Blessing focus on how we relate to our immediate environment and to the web of personal connections we have through family, friends, work, vocation, and the like.

The skill of Holding relates to the Cup and Space metaphor we have explored previously. Holding is what a cup does. Holding is what space makes possible. We talk a lot about holding. We say, "I will hold you in my heart," or "I'll hold you in mind." Just what do these expressions mean? What actually are we doing when we "hold" someone "in our heart"? What are we doing when we hold them in our minds? Is this just a poetic way of saying that we care for them and will remember them? A person might say, "God holds us in love." What does that mean? What is God doing in such an instance? What does that do to us? Holding someone in love or in "our hearts" is different than a cup holding coffee or a bathtub holding hot water. Or is it? A key point is to realize that holding is a power, a capacity, and one that can have surprising results. Like standing, it is something we can overlook because it seems so ordinary and familiar.

For me, Holding is the foundation of blessing, another spiritual capacity we all have. I differentiate between two kinds of blessing, generally speaking. (Actually, there are as many kinds of blessings as there are situations to bless and people to do the blessing!) One is where we provide energy or qualities of some kind appropriate to the situation. For example, I might send love to someone who is having a hard time, or hold that person in love in my heart and mind. The other is where I simply hold the person without qualifying what should happen, what kind of energies should be involved, and so on. In this second form, there is no agenda. I think of these two types of blessings in this way: if my youngest daughter has had a hard day at school and is feeling blue, I can hold her on my lap and just let her cry it out or talk it out or whatever she needs. My job is to be a presence that creates a space in which she can do what she needs to do. On the other hand, there may be something specifically the matter where I can offer advice or counsel or perhaps she needs help with her homework. Then there is some specific quality or help that I can offer. With respect to blessing, there are times when we can offer something specific. It might be our time, words of advice, money, or some needed quality. But much of the time, the soul of the other person (or persons) knows what is needed and just needs a protective space in which to seek it out. I think of this kind of blessing as giving the soul elbowroom, free of interfering psychic or subtle energies from the world, in which to discover how it can bless itself. Let's explore this in a variant of the exercise we have already done.

Notes and Reflections

Exercise Seven: The Lap

Like the first exercise on Standing, this is also a physical exercise. But this time it involves an equally familiar and simple procedure: sitting down and forming a lap. A lap is a physical form of holding. It is the form of a cup, a bowl, a cauldron, or a grail. Imagine kids climbing into a lap: it is a place of love, comfort, healing, and transformation. In this exercise, simply sit down and form a lap. Go through the following elements as you do so, exploring the felt sense of each. Inherent in the lap is your power of holding which is at the heart of blessing.

Physical:

The physical action of this exercise is simplicity itself and the opposite of the Standing exercise. From a standing position, you simply sit down, allowing your legs to form a lap. Be aware of the physical sensation and felt sense of being a lap. Feel the relaxation of sitting but at the same time the power and receptivity of forming a lap. Explore the felt sense of the space that is created in front of you, around you, and within you when you sit and form a lap.

Emotional:

Feel the power of being a space of holding. In your sovereignty, you are forming a space of comfort, a space of healing, a space of encouragement and upliftment. In this space, negativity can be received and transformed as you hold a presence of peace, of love, and of strength.

Mental:

Your mind is also a lap. It is a cup that holds your thoughts. As you sit, let your mind go beyond the contents of any thoughts you may be holding. Let it simply appreciate the space within it. Let your mind fill with that space. If thoughts come within it, simply welcome them and let them sit in your mind-lap for a time, then move on. Remember, you are holding them, they are not holding you. You create and own the space they occupy. Sit in that space, be at peace, and feel the power of your mind to be a lap.

Magical:

The cup is the oldest of magical images. It is the grail of the sacred, the cauldron of magic and wisdom, and the cooking pot that creates nourishment, the womb of life, the space that holds the cosmos. Your lap is this space, this grail, this cauldron, this womb, and this cup. When you sit and a lap is formed, you are in resonance with the place where transformation can take place and new life is born.

Spiritual:

Sitting, your lap is the presence of the sacred. It is a place of love, a place to receive and comfort pain and suffering, a place of healing. In the space of your lap you are in resonance with the primal space that holds all things and allows them to be. God is a lap!

In doing this exercise, you sit and as you do so, work through these levels of sensation, feeling, thought, energy, and spirit, appreciating the power, the freedom, the sovereignty, and the presence emerging from the simple act of forming a lap.

Notes and Reflections

Exercise Eight:
The Sphere of Holding and Blessing

In this Exercise, we are repeating the sitting exercise but adding one element to it. This time we will visualize a bubble of Light resting on our lap. Within this bubble we will place whatever we wish to hold and bless. Sit and form a lap as before. This time, in the space of the lap imagine a bubble forming. It can be any size that feels appropriate and comfortable. Let this bubble simply be an open space, unconditioned but held with strength and love. Imagine in the bubble a person or situation to whom or to which you would like to offer a blessing. On the outside of the bubble, let words form that represent a specific kind of blessing if you have one, but allow the interior of the bubble to be free of expectation. That which is in the bubble can draw upon the wishes and energies you place on the outside if it wishes. Otherwise just let it be in a space that allows this person or situation to find the right activity, the right movement, the right choices, that will manifest its own capacity to bless itself and attune to its highest good. Hold the bubble as long as it feels comfortable. When you feel tired or restless or feel that the blessing has accomplished its end, see the bubble returning to an empty state and then let it dissolve, taking its energy with it.

Practice A+B

Let's add this Holding exercise into the Practice sequence we're building up. Begin with a moment of Standing, gaining a felt sense of all that means for you, then letting that felt sense lead you into attuning and standing in your Self-Light, appreciating all that means to you and feeling how that lives in your body and in your heart and mind. From a standing position, sit down, creating a lap. This lap is symbolic of your power to Hold and to Bless. Imagine a bubble forming and resting in your lap. This bubble is formed from your Self-Light in concert and harmony with whatever Light you would draw from other spiritual sources meaningful to you. Take a moment to hold within this bubble the elements of the day that is starting. Hold the people you may meet, the places you will go, and the tasks you will be doing. Extend to each of them the blessings of this Light, and Hold each of them in a space of no agenda in which there is psychological, psychic, energetic, and spiritual room for new possibilities to unfold, for your inner capacities to be fully expressed, for blessing to manifest. Then open your bubble to anything else you might wish to be Held by you in your Self-Light and attunement. When you feel complete, let your bubble open and let its Light flow freely and expansively out into your world. Record your experiences on the following pages or in your journal.

Notes and Reflections

Chapter Five
The Incarnational Field

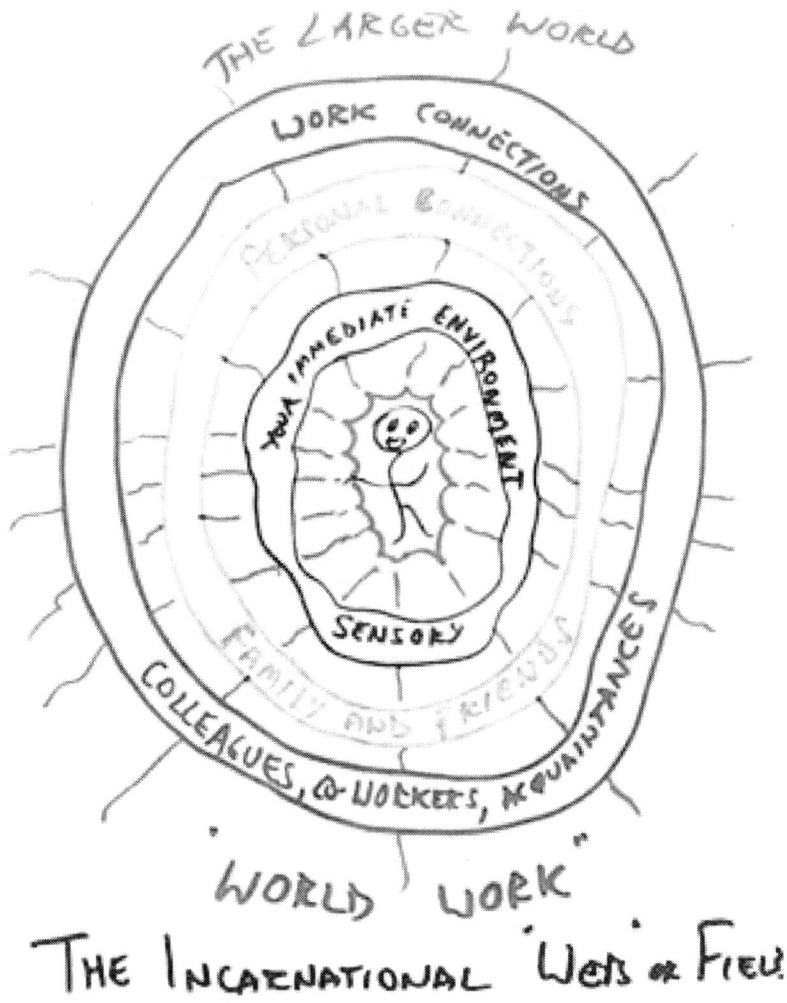

The Incarnational Web or Field

    The picture which begins this chapter conveys (in stunningly beautiful graphics, of course!) the idea of each of us being at the center of a web of interactions and relationships that are concrete and specific to each of us. This is a cluster of relationships and interactions that I call the "Incarnational Field." It is meant to be suggestive, not definitive.

You may experience elements in your Field that are not shown in this diagram. Each of us is both the center of our own web of relationships and connections, and a part of the webs of others' connections. We have our own incarnational field and we participate in and are part of the incarnational fields of others. In the TV reality show 'Survivor," a group of people are placed in some remote environment like an isolated island and have to both work together and to compete to survive for about 36 days. Every three days someone is voted out of the group until at the end only one person remains the "Survivor," who wins a million dollars. The motto of this show is "Outwit, Outplay, Outlast." Incarnational Spirituality has an equivalent motto that describes its objectives: "connect, engage, and emerge." So our Individuality and Sovereignty are part of the incarnate world to connect, to engage, and to create possibilities and openings for emergence.

The Incarnational Field represents the personal dimension of our connection and engagement with the larger world. It represents the cluster of people and places and energies that are directly and consistently in connection and engagement with us. It provides the environment and opportunities for the most immediate and sustained expression of your personal energies and spirit. If your body provides incarnation to your private, personal self, your incarnational field provides incarnation to your collective, relational self. In the picture, I have layered this field into three levels. The boundaries between them are not hard and fast. This is as much a rhetorical distinction as it is one in the actual world, a way of describing what this field is. You should define your incarnational field and what is in it in your own unique way, which might be the same as I am doing but could be quite different. These levels represent where your energy goes and what it connects to and engages with most of the time.

Level of Physical Environmental

The first level or layer or strand in the web is your immediate physical and subtle environment that's right there for your senses to perceive. For instance, I look around and I see my computer, a computer desk, a bookshelf with books and CDs, a living room with chairs, sofa, a fireplace, and a television. This physical environment (and its subtle, non-physical energy counterpart) is what is receiving the radiation of my energy that I'm generating and being a source of right now. In its own way this immediate, sensory and meta-sensory environment is a cradle that is holding you. It is a cup and space in its own right.

Your energy interacts with it in a ways that creates a particular atmosphere or mood that is a vibrational environment. There is no doubt that our physical environment shapes our incarnations in various ways. If I live in a desert, my life will be different than if I live in arctic tundra. I once met two spiritual teachers from very different parts of the world. One was a Native American from the deserts of the Southwest. He was lean and tan and wrinkled and looked like an old shoe that a coyote had gnawed on and spit out. There wasn't a bit of fat on him. He was all sinew and bone. On the podium with him was a shaman from Polynesia. He was large and fat, his skin smooth and light, and he reminded me of a pale beach ball that had become a Buddha. Seeing the two of them together, one from the desert, the other from the sea, was sheer delight. And you could see how who they were and what they were had been shaped by their environments.

Level of Family, Friends and Personal Relationship

This layer and the one that follows are separated not by distance but by intimacy. A different kind of energy exists between ourselves and those with whom we have ties of blood, genetics, love, friendship, and intimacy, and those who are strangers to us or casual acquaintances. This layer is a relational body that shapes our incarnation. It is a sphere of activity, through which we connect, engage, and emerge.

Level of Collegiality, Work, and Teachers

This layer, which like the second one is relational in nature, is less intimate than the second is, generally speaking. If a co-worker or teacher is also a close friend and has a deeper, more lasting affect upon us, then that person would energetically be part of the second layer, not this third one. Yet there is no doubt we are shaped in our incarnations by the people we work with, the tasks we perform, and often by individuals whom we may not know well, if at all, but who have been influential teachers, mentors, coaches, and inspirations for us.

These three layers form our Incarnational Field, like an energetic web or sphere around us. Metaphorically, it might be considered a "body" through which we engage with the world. From an inner worlds' point of view, this is more than a metaphor. We truly "co-incarnate" each other and carry each other's energies into expression in a variety of ways. It could be said that anyone who reads something I've written, is inspired by it, and turns that inspiration into some form of action is carrying my energy into further incarnation in ways that I could not. But it is also true that I become part of their Field of Incarnation. This is obviously true with people with whom we are close or in regular interaction. My presence is a strong factor in how my children are shaping their incarnations, just as they shape mine. This is the essence of co- incarnation.

These Fields of Incarnation can be considered as "force multipliers," as well. They take our personal energies and magnify them and distribute them, as in the example I made of my writing. But there could be so many examples, both positive and negative, of how these webs of relationship distribute their energy throughout the entire field. If I am a loving father, that loving energy moves through my kids' lives and on into their friends' lives. It may cease to be consciously associated with me, and it certainly gets mixed up in an alchemical brew of energies and qualities coming from many different sources, but I am still part of it. There comes a point, an invisible membrane or boundary that would be very difficult to fix, when direct association with our energy peters out. Now the energy itself may not do so, but a person tracing it back might not arrive at me. I am not so much a source as a contributor or participant, if that is a clear distinction. Where that boundary is becomes the limit of my Field of Incarnation. I think of this boundary as metaphorically similar to that of the earth's atmosphere. There is no hard wall that keeps the air in. We are not floating in space like a giant, planet-size spaceship or Dyson sphere. Instead, the atmosphere just becomes thinner and thinner, the gaseous molecules further and further apart until eventually for all practical purposes one is in the vacuum of space.

There is another side to this Field that the picture does not show, as it is focused primarily upon our physical human relationships, mainly with other humans. This Field is really like a sphere. Part of it extends into nature and the earth and all the spiritual forces that work with the earth; the other part extends into what we usually call the spiritual or "higher" realms of angels and spiritual guides and teachers, and the realm of the Soul. (Note that in my cosmology the Sacred is neither up, down, or in the middle, but fills and holds the entire sphere.) There is a whole part of Incarnational Spirituality, which I call working with Alliances. This part deals with working with non-physical parts of the Incarnational Field (or Incarnational Sphere), which forms a class on its own. I want to mention it so that when you think of this Field you can have a more rounded picture of it than the diagram I drew above fully offers. The Incarnational Field is one of the ways my unique energy moves out into the world. So I want to relate to my "cluster" or "web" of the people, places, and things that participate in my Field, as I do in theirs in a way that enhances its capacity to truly represent my energy.

This is as simple as saying that if I want my presence on earth to manifest a loving energy, then I want to enhance the chance that my Field and all within it will also express this loving energy. I can't do this by trying to control everyone; that would have the opposite effect! I cannot bring them into or under my Sovereignty. I need to honor and respect theirs. What it does mean is that when dealing with, thinking about or feeling into the participants in my Field, I want to do that in a way that enhances the possibilities and emergence of a loving spirit. This is no different in principle from creating a shared spirit within a department at work or within a team, though it *is* different in operation. Most people in my Field don't think of themselves as part of "David's Department" or "David's Team," though they may think of me as being part of theirs. They do think of them and me as being partners in some manner, whether it is friendship, mutual knowledge, shared values, or common goals.

An Incarnational Field is not simply a metaphor. From an inner perspective, it is an "energetic object." It is, well, an actual field. And it can be nourished. Indeed, I think that such nourishment is part of a regular spiritual practice, as much as energy hygiene or attunement to the sacred or standing in one's Self-Light. That is what the following exercise is about. I may be part of many people's incarnational field, but it is my field, the one I am at the center of, that is my accountability. If we are mutual friends and we are both part of each other's Incarnational Field, then my concern is not what you are doing with your field but what I do with mine. I need be concerned about how I connect and engage with you but I can't expect to control or manipulate how you connect and engage with me. A person's Sovereignty can support an Incarnational Field but one does not dominate it. Think of your Incarnational Field as a tool or mode of incarnation, as another way of bringing your Soul energy, your Self-Light, your Blessing, into the world, one that potentially do so with greater power than you can do on your own.

As people in the future become more aware of and conversant with subtle energies and more aware of the spiritual, magical, and energetic dynamics of incarnation, in addition to the physical, we will learn how to work more co-creatively, mindfully, and gracefully with these Fields. Then they can become truly powerful and coherent contributions to the world. It is most definitely not that everyone has to behave the same, think the same, or be the same. It's not a reversion to older tribal cohesion. But it is the beginning of a kind of relationship jazz in which we blend our unique individual skills of incarnation of connection, engagement, and emergence improvisational with those with whom we are close—the participants in our various fields. We will riff off each other and learning to hear melodies that arise from all of us in order to create whole new music for the blessing of the earth.

Notes and Reflections

Exercise Nine: Holding and Blessing Your Incarnational Field

This is a simple exercise, but it is one that you can expand and tweak in a variety of ways. The principle is an extension of the Holding exercise. In this case you are Holding yourself and your perceptions, thoughts, and feelings about people in your Incarnational Field. Then you are extending a blessing of some nature out into that Field. The idea is to first affect your own relationship with and perception of those who most connect and engage with your own incarnation and have the most affect upon you. Next, turn that perception into a blessing for them. The principle is that when your perceptions, thoughts, expectations, and feelings towards and about others are Held in your own Self-Light and in the love, compassion, joy, and sacredness that are part of that Light, then something changes in the relationship. The relationship becomes more radiant and clear in its own way, more translucent and conductive of that Light, more honoring and nourishing of the Sovereignty and Self- Light within others in your Field. You are not working on them to change in anyway. You are working on yourself and changing yourself in relationship to them. This will have an effect.

The second part of the exercise is more projective in that you are mindfully altering the energy characteristics of the Field you form with the people closest to you or the ones who have the most influence upon your own incarnation. You are taking steps to uplift and uphold their own sovereignty, their own standing, their own will-to-be, their own participation in the incarnational process, all as part of your participation in the co-incarnational, co-creative connection you share with these people, places, and things.

Part 1

Begin with Standing, gaining the felt sense of your Self-Light and internal generative radiance. Then sit and picture a bubble forming in your lap, as in the Blessing variant of the previous exercise. Let this bubble expand around you so you are at its center. Let it expand to fill the room you are in. If you are outdoors, or the space around you seems too large to encompass, then let the bubble expand to about six feet or a body length around you on all sides. Fill this bubble with the radiance of your Self-Light. If you wish to align this with the Light of any other sacred or spiritual source that is meaningful to you, then please do so. With your eyes open, let your perception roam about the room or environment immediately around you. Let everything you see around you, above you, and below you be embraced by this bubble and Held within it, becoming part of its radiance.

Close your eyes and imagine other physical places that are important to you, where you spend time and that form regular parts of your life. You don't have to imagine them in detail, just sufficiently to feel the felt sense of that place as if you were in it or in contact with it now. Let your felt sense of your immediate environment and the environments you are imagining impress itself like symbols or pictures or engravings on the inside of your bubble.

Now imagine members of your family, friends, and people who are close to you: those who you would place in the second circle of your field. You don't have to imagine everyone. You can let two or three people represent this dimension of connection and engagement, or you can remember and name as many as you wish. The object is to feel the felt sense of them, the way in which you relate to them whether positively or negatively.

Once you have a sense of your bubble filled with the spirits of these close friends and family, surrounded by your Light, let the felt sense of them impress them upon the inner wall of your bubble as if they are symbols or engravings or pictures. The bubble itself is now empty, but the inside of your bubble holds the images of your relationship with these people just as it does the images of your relationship with your physical environment.

Now repeat this exercise with those who would be part of your third layer, those with whom you work, colleagues, people who are not intimately related to you as family or friends, people whom you see everyday or regularly and who affect your life in meaningful ways. Again, draw them into the bubble and the Light it contains and as before, think of two or three people who represent the intention that they stand for all the others as well. As before, let the Light impress the felt sense of your relationship with them as images or engravings upon the inner wall of your bubble.

Now imagine yourself in your bubble, and along its interior are all these images representing the points of connection, engagement, emergence, and relationship with places, people, and things that are mostly closely and co-creatively linked with you and your incarnation. You want to have a sense of them as an energy field surrounding you and interacting with you. From your own point of Sovereignty and Self-Light, let Light flow into all these images, turning them translucent and clear, cleaning them, clarifying them, opening them to greater flow, filling them with love, compassion, maybe forgiveness if that seems appropriate, and a willing supportiveness. What you are clearing and cleaning and filling with Light are the thought forms, images, preconceptions, expectations, and memories that form and shape the images you hold of these people, places, and things. By doing so, you are opening these relationships to a more direct engagement with your Self-Light and with theirs as well. You are turning your incarnational field into a presence of co-creative and loving energy for all whom are parts, and freeing yourself to encounter and engage with these places, people, and things in new and exciting ways.

Part 2

At the center of your bubble, whose inside is now clear, let your Self-Light flow out and connect with those who are part of your Incarnational Field. Let this Light flow through the purified and translucent images of your relationships with these people, places, and things. Imagine this Light flowing through your point of connection with them into their own unique Incarnational Fields, bringing clarity, blessing, and Light into their own lives in ways they can use according to their own needs and will. You can name any quality you would like to share through this Light. It could be love, joy, courage, peace, or whatever you wish. You are not imposing this quality, but you are offering it into their Fields through their connections with you, and it passes through your own cleansed and clarified Field in a clear, pure, open way that does not simply project your own stuff onto them.

When you feel this is complete, then simply let your bubble

dissolve the Light within it being released into the world. Do whatever seems right to you to ground yourself and bring yourself gracefully back into sovereignty, integrity, and wholeness with your everyday life. Record in your journal your experiences with this exercise.

This exercise can seem elaborate, and it certainly takes more words to describe it than it takes time to do it. The important thing is to understand what you are doing and why, and to feel the felt sense in your body of each step. Then you can move through this exercise very quickly, or you can redesign it completely to fit your own style and uniqueness. A key thought is that the images and feelings you hold of a person, based on the dynamics of your relationship with him or her, past history, and the like, can influence energetically how you interact with this person. In this exercise, you are initially using the concept of the Incarnational Field to Hold this person <u>and</u> your images of him or her and then transform them so they give no impediment or distortion to the flow of Light between you. You are cleaning the soot off the inside of your lantern. This will have an energetic effect on everyone involved, and you personally may well find it very liberating of your own energy. With that in mind, please feel free to experiment. After all, exercises are made for you, not you for the exercise! Be sure to record in the space provided or in your journal your experiences with this exercise.

Practice AB+C

Let's add this Holding and Radiating exercise into the Practice sequence we're building up. Begin with a moment of Standing, gaining a felt sense of all that means for you, then letting that felt sense lead you into attuning and standing in your Self-Light, appreciating all that means to you and feeling how that lives in your body and in your heart and mind.

From a standing position, sit down, creating a lap. This lap is symbolic of your power to Hold and to Bless. Imagine a bubble forming and resting in your lap. This bubble is formed from your Self-Light in concert and harmony with whatever Light you would draw from other spiritual sources meaningful to you. Take a moment to Hold within this bubble the layers of your Incarnational Field and the people, places, and things it embraces, just as you did above.

Then, when this feels complete, hold the elements of the day that is starting: the people you may meet, the places you will go, and the tasks you will be doing. Extend to each of them the blessings of this Light, and Hold each of them in an agenda-less space in which there is psychological, psychic, energetic, and spiritual room for new possibilities to unfold, for your inner capacities to be fully expressed, for blessing to manifest.

When you feel complete, let your bubble open and let its Light flow freely and expansively out into your world.

Notes and Reflections

Chapter Six
Touching the Earth

The first level of incarnational involvement is with ourselves. The second is with our immediate environment and the circle of people and places directly connected to us in some way or another. The third is with the world as a whole. Incarnational Spirituality is not only about personal incarnation. It is about world incarnation as well and the incarnational process within all life. It is about being an agent that contributes positively to that process. We call this "world work."

There are many ways of doing world work. We can be activists on different fronts: political, economic, ecological, and social. We can volunteer our services to our communities in various capacities. We can donate time, energy, money, and work to causes that inspire us. We can care for the land we live on, conserve the energy we use, buy smart, and many other things. When we do these things standing in our Self-Light, with integrity and sovereignty, and are conscious of being a source of spiritual radiance, we bring a whole new dimension to our contributions.

There are also ways of doing inner world work. The most common of these, practiced by people in churches, synagogues, mosques, temples, and homes throughout the world is through prayer. But from our Self-Light and its connection and resonance with Light from other spiritual and planetary sources we can also do various forms of energy work, altering and affecting the energy environment or conditions of planetary situations. When I think of world work, I think of the act of Holding writ large, Holding directed towards situations and people in my neighborhood, city, country or the global community.

There can be more to it than just Holding, but Holding is where it starts for me. Remember that Holding is a mental, emotional, and spiritual embrace of a situation that is initially without agenda save to create a spaciousness, an openness in which deeper processes of blessing and spirit have room and opportunity to come into play. Other, more energetic activities can follow on if appropriate. In the exercise for world work, I will be using our sense of touch to concretely engage with the world around us but with that touch also carrying the energy and felt sense of Holding as you've experienced it in the previous exercises.

Touching is the transmission of our influence into the world. It is the transmission of our energy and the inner qualities we are carrying. There are many ways in which we touch the world around us. Most of them are non-physical. We do so with our eyes; we do so with our ears. We touch with our thoughts, our feelings, and our attitudes. And this touch does have an effect. (For an interesting take on this phenomenon, see Daniel Goleman's book, Social Intelligence.) It is easy to see how, as in the previous exercise; we can directly influence our immediate surroundings and connections through our energies since we are so obviously "in touch" with them. But what about influencing the world as a whole? What about influencing events transpiring on the other side of the earth? How can we touch them? What influence do we have on persons and places dozens, hundreds, or thousands of miles away? I can only speak from my own experience and observations.

The key lies, in fact, in touching itself, in the condition that everything is part of a chain or sphere of touching that links all phenomena together. One may define or experience this chain or sphere of connectedness in different ways. For example, I might experience it as a flow of energy that links me to wherever and whomever my attention and intent is directed. I may experience it as participating in an interconnected, interdependent holism. I might also experience it as being connected through intermediaries, such as angelic beings that pick up my inner touch and take its qualities to wherever they are needed. I may be connected through an entirely unknown (as yet) level of order and organization within the universe such as manifests through synchronicity and coincidence. I might be connected through laws of quantum relationship, such as entanglement and non-locality. The point is that I don't have to know how it works. I simply need to know that it can work, that the Self-Light and blessings I generate as a source can reach out into my world and contribute to the healing, balancing, comforting, nourishing, fostering, and upholding of situations far distant from me. This leads us to the next exercise.

Notes and Reflections

Exercise Ten:
The Holding Touch

Begin this exercise with Standing and then sit and, forming a lap, shift to Holding. Feel the open space and power of your Holding. You may, if you wish, visualize it as a bubble of Light and energy, as in previous exercises.

Once you have the felt sense of this Holding firmly in your mind and body, then imagine this bubble or sense of Holding moving down both your arms and splitting into ten smaller "bubbles" or expressions of Holding, one moving into the tip of each finger. Imagine your hands as cups, and then your fingers, as if at the end of each finger is a lap, a cup, and a power of Holding.

Now get up and move about your room. Touch things. Take a moment with each thing you touch to feel it being held by the loving, holding power at your fingertips. Visualize each touch surrounding that which you are touching with a bubble of openness, creating spaciousness within which blessings may arise from within that which you are touching itself. Pay attention to the felt sense of this at your fingertips, as well as within your body as a whole. Each "fingercup," each "fingerlap," is empowered by your Self-Light and by the Light of any other sacred source with which you may wish to partner. Each finger's touch awakens the possibility of blessing and spaciousness.

Once you have in mind the felt sense of this, you can manifest this touch of Holding anytime, with any one or any thing, during the day. A simple handshake can become a moment of blessing. Remember that energy is NOT flowing from your hands into another. Instead, your fingers create a space of Holding for the other within which their own life, their own Soul, their own beingness, can find room to generate the blessing. Nor is energy flowing back into you from whatever or whomever you are touching. Your fingers are helping them to become a cup to hold their own blessings, not being a cup to receive and hold their energies.

If you feel energy flowing back into you, just see it being held at your fingertips and offered back. This is <u>not</u> an exercise in giving and receiving energy but of Holding and creating a space for blessing to emerge. If at any time this activity of Holding feels tiresome or uncomfortable, just feel the power of Holding moving back up your hand and arms away from your fingers, and back into the core of your being, into your Self- Light. It will be held there until you wish to extend it again. Take a few moments to record your experiences.

Notes and Reflections

Exercise Eleven:
Massaging the World

Sometimes when I have bodywork done, the person working on me cannot get to the actual tight places that are the origin of my distress. But she or he can work on muscles that are closer to the surface and by loosening them, set up a cascade of relaxation that does affect the deeper, sore places, relieving their tension. In a similar way, I use a wonderful tool consisting entirely of two specially designed, rubbery balls. I put the balls on the floor and I lie on them, positioning them under muscles that feel tight. I then just lie there on my back on the balls, letting gravity do the work as I relax. It is a technique that relaxes all the muscles of my body, not just the ones under the balls. The release of tension in one place triggers the release of tension in other places.

At the moment, our world is a very tense place with very tight human "muscles." The tightness and constriction of the energetic environment caused by fear, suffering, anger, hatred, conflict, and violence blocks and disrupts the natural renewing and healing energies of the earth. I cannot travel to Korea and negotiate peace between North Korea and the United States. I can touch the earth in a way that contributes to other efforts being made by physical and non-physical beings to relax the tension in that area, or in the Middle East, or elsewhere around the world. That is the sense of this exercise, using the metaphor of massage.

Exercise

Enter into your own inner states of Self-Light, Sovereignty, and Holding. In these states, feel any tension you have relax and fade away. Release judgments, fears, angers, tensions you have toward any person or place on the earth so that you have a felt sense of being strong, resilient, in balance, and grounded. You are Held by spiritual forces to which you attune, and filled with the power of your own capacity to Hold. When you feel comfortable in such a state, then reach out and touch something that is connected to the earth. If you are outside (an ideal place for doing this), touch the soil beneath you. If you are inside touch anything. In the web of connectedness in which we move everything is ultimately connected to the earth. You can touch a chair that touches the floor that touches the walls that touch the foundation that touches the earth. You can lie on the floor and feel your energy flowing down the walls, into the foundations, and into the earth. Whatever route of connection you take, imagine yourself touching the earth.

As before, feel each of your fingertips becoming a cup of Holding. Feel your whole body being a cup of Holding. In this Holding you are providing a spaciousness within which constricted energies can relax and lose their tension, becoming supple and flowing again. In this relaxed and flowing state, connection can be made with other energies in the world but also, importantly, with the dynamic, flowing, nurturing, healing, blessing energies of the spiritual worlds and of the Sacred. This opens connection with the natural healing and restorative powers within the earth and within humanity. As you feel this spaciousness opening up around your touch and moving deeper and outward into the earth and into the world of humanity, turn your attention and your intent to contribute to some area of the world where you feel the energies to be constricted and tight. You may not be in direct touch with this place from where you are, but the world is in touch with it, and you are in touch with the world. The world listens and responds to your touch.

You don't have to do any work other than to hold this open space of blessing and touch. The deep spirit of the earth knows what to do. The deep spirit of humanity knows what to do. If you feel inspired to offer a prayer or thought for blessing, for healing, for specific help for a specific place or person or situation, then do so. But remember, it's not your task to impose, even if you feel you know what the situation needs. If you project a specific energy, it may be well-received but it may be rejected, and if the latter happens, the constriction and tightness will return as the situation, person or place defends itself against your intrusion. This is why we work with forces of spaciousness, holding, and relaxation. We let the healing power of the Whole have room and an opportunity to become active and let the constricting energies of fear, pain, suffering, loss, anger, and grief have a chance to open up. Then they can be released into the larger flow of love that arises from the heart of the world and the hearts of our own Souls.

So feel your touch massaging with love and spaciousness the part of the earth you can touch. Feel your touch Holding and inspiring openness and flow, letting the healing powers of spirit and earth a chance to work their wonders in the area or situation to which you are directing your attention and intent.

When you feel restless or tired or distracted, then bring this session to a close. Feel the earth touching you back with grace and love, cleansing you of any constricting energies you may have touched into or picked up, or which you may have carried in yourself. Stand and reaffirm your Sovereignty. Stand in your Self-Light. Hold yourself in peace and spaciousness. Then step into your day. Take some time to record your experiences below or in your journal.

Notes and Reflections

Chapter Seven
Summation

Incarnational Spirituality is ultimately about changing your world. We may not have talked about change a lot, but the fact is when we change ourselves, we change our world. It is one of the most profound acts of world work we can undertake. In creating this introduction to Incarnational Spirituality, I had three levels of change in mind. One is the change in my personal worldview. Change comes when I understand that I am a sacred being, that incarnation is ok and is itself a sacred act. Change comes when I understand that I am a source of spiritual radiance as an incarnate person, and that there is a Self-Light which I can offer to the world in participation with the Light and sacredness already in the world and in the cosmos as a whole.

The second level of change happens when I extend that Light, in the form of Holding and blessing, out into my immediate relational web or sphere, those people, places, and things who in one way or another, to a greater or lesser degree, are my co-incarnates. They are helping to shape who I am and they are, in turn, shaped by my participation in their lives and beingness. This relational web, which I termed the Incarnational Field, in itself acts as a collective, communal incarnation on a small scale. Its boundaries are fluid and wave-like. Change at that level can affect many people, many places, and many things.

The third level is world change. Most of us are not in positions of global economic, political, or scientific power and influence. Still, we are part of the whole, and our energy moves through the wholeness of the world in unexpected and influential ways. We can be like the fabled butterfly the beating of whose wings sets a storm in motion half a world away. I have treated all of these three levels of change and engagement in what I hope have been simple and straightforward ways, though in fact the material can take us to surprising depths.

To round this off, I wanted to share some thoughts about incarnation itself as a world work. From my point of view, we each come into this world with four primary connections. We are connected to our selves, to our own unique flow of identity and being and we are connected to spirit. We are also connected to humanity, to the earth and to nature. All of these connections might also be seen as aspects of a deeper connection to the holism of the world, the world system as a whole. This is analogous to saying that each of us has body, heart, mind, and spirit, but that no one of these is the true Self. We are the holism that these four spheres of connection come together and create. Each of these connections is an aspect or a part of a larger state of being and identity which we can experience when we can bring these four aspects into coherency and balance. The process of incarnation, the process of being, connecting, engaging, and emerging, can be seen as well as a process of bringing these four connections together. The result is that we, and through us, the world, experiences the holism of this world. It is an experience of spaciousness and inclusivity that is itself a Cup and a Space within which we can all Hold and be Held in new ways that are healing and full of blessing.

The challenge our world faces is that we identify with one or two of these connections and not with the others. We pull apart the wholeness of the world. We shatter its incarnational coherency and process. So if I am a materialist, I say yes to body, yes to nature and the earth, yes to humanity, but no to spirit. If I am an environmentalist, I may say yes to nature but no to humanity. If I am a technologist, I may say yes to humanity and no to nature. We pull these four elements apart as individuals too. We may, in the category of Self, say yes to body but no to spirit, or vice versa. In the category of Humanity, we may say yes to being an American or a Christian or a Republican and no to being a North Korean or a Moslem or a Democrat. We fail in our connections. Consequently, we fail in engaging in full and holistic ways, not to mention in loving and compassionate ways. Imagine what might emerge, what could emerge, what possibilities and potentials might be actualized if we humans lived in peace with each other. Instead, we become locked in closed, self-repeating systems of attitude, opinion, worldview, belief, and behavior, through which the sins of the fathers are indeed visited upon the children.

This is why a non-physical being who was a colleague of mine for many years said, "It's not that humanity is too incarnated; the problem is that you are not incarnated enough!" That statement, for me, set into motion the impetus to develop an Incarnational Spirituality. I see a spirituality that in its fullness focuses both on individual development, salvation or progress and on collective development. Incarnational Spirituality gives us the tools to become agents and artists of incarnation so that we may bring the incarnation of the world system into its wholeness and fullest expression.

Incarnational Spirituality is part of a larger phenomenon that to me is very important. That is the phenomenon of emergent spirituality. Emergent spirituality is more than new forms of spirituality appearing or that we are be entering a post-traditional age in which some people are asking "What's next?" Emergent spirituality is more than a new revelation or the teachings of the next prophet or messiah. It is the realization that spirituality is itself an emergent phenomenon. This does not and need not diminish the power and usefulness of traditions. It does affirm the source-ness within us each and the improvisational nature of spirit. It is not that each of us becomes a prophet and pronounces our own private revelations. Rather, it is that spirit lives in the emergent moment. Just as we cannot define God, the Sacred, the Generative Mystery, or the Unmanifest, so we cannot predict just how that sacredness should or may emerge in the moment that is just beginning. The conditions and players in that moment haven't existed in that combination ever before. Who knows what possibilities may erupt or appear if we are willing and open for that to happen? This is the emergence part of incarnation.

Emergent spirituality is partly about the appearance of new spiritual understandings and insights that happen as we continue to evolve. It is also a realization that spirituality emerges from us and from our capacities and nature as a source. It is not just something that is passed down to us, given to us, or laid out as an unchanging path that we must follow. This puts an emphasis upon who we are and what we are doing in the moment. What is emerging from us, from our hearts and minds, from our activities, from our souls? It makes spirituality person-centered as well as God-centered. Each person holds the power to determine whether the sacred will emerge through his or her actions and presence each moment or not. As we connect and engage with others and with the world, will compassion emerge? Will love emerge? Will wisdom emerge? Will fostering and empowerment emerge? Will honoring emerge?

We each have an incarnational power to determine what will

emerge, and this power can be developed, nurtured, strengthened, and attuned with practice. This power ultimately is what will doom or save our world. It is far more powerful than any atomic bomb, any disease organism, or any chemical weapon. This is the power that determines whether or not we choose to use these things upon each other. It is the experience and development of this power in attunement with the holism of ourselves, our humanity, and our world that is the calling of an emergent, incarnational spirituality.

Can we be better incarnated than we are? There is much evidence that the answer is yes. A friend just gave me Arjuna Ardagh's book, <u>The Translucent Revelation</u>. It is an account based on the author's travels around our planet interviewing hundreds of people. It is about the ways in which consciousness is changing, unfolding, and perceiving in new, emergent ways, and how that relatively unseen but very powerful movement is changing the world.

In my own work, I see people changing all the time, and I can see how that change has accelerated in the past few years. I have been teaching since 1964, and I can definitely say that the consciousness of the people I work with now is much more advanced, open, ready, and able than it was forty-two years ago, even with people who are encountering ideas of emergent spirituality for the first time. I have tremendous hope for our future. This future flows in important and vital ways not from higher levels of spirit or from hierarchies of Masters or Ascended Beings but from our own incarnations, particularly as we experience and develop the spiritual power of incarnation itself.

May your incarnations be richly blessed and open to bring you each moment to your fullest expression.

David Spangler

Notes and Reflections

What's Next?

We hope that you enjoyed and benefited from what you have engaged so far. Though designed to be complete in itself, this Textbook is also part of a larger developing program. There is much more to Incarnational Spirituality overall.

The Lorian Association through the Lorian center for Incarnational Spirituality offers a variety of mechanisms to support the practices suggested by this book.

In addition, Incarnational Spirituality is an evolving study. We encourage you to explore and experiment and, if you wish, to share what you discover with the larger Lorian community. In this way, Incarnational Spirituality can grow and benefit from the ongoing experience and insights of all of us who wish to see the world benefit from its contributions.

If you wish to proceed, what's next? We have tried to provide several options so you can interact with the material in a variety of ways depending on your life situation. Here are some of those options:

1. View, listen to, or read any of the DVD's, audio CD's, website articles, and booklets available free and through the web from Lorian.

2. Sign up for Lorian's free e-newsletter and/or David Spangler's periodic e-articles. Simply go to www.lorian.org and click on the newsletter sign up button on the home page. And, while you're there browse through some of the other articles, information and links on our website. If you are on our mailing list, you will receive every two weeks an article from David Spangler called "David's Desk," a monthly e-newsletter, and announcements about special activities and classes.

3. Engage in a program of self directed learning using material produced by the Lorian Center for Incarnational Spirituality (shown below).

4. You may also wish to connect with a group in your area studying Lorian material or form a study group yourself. Lorian is available to supply materials and support. These include:

Incarnational Spirituality: *A strategy to bless our World* (This textbook) An introduction to Incarnational Spirituality by David Spangler $15.

Embodying Eden: Roots of a New Culture A workbook on Loving Self, Others, World, and Actions by Jeremy Berg $15.

Manifestation: Creating the life you love – Card Deck and Manual by David Spangler $25. This book and deck can also be purchased with four audio CD's covering an introductory talk and one day workshop on Manifestation by David for $55.

The Starshaman Home Mystery School™ Series by David Spangler. These Four Modules cover the foundations of Incarnational Spirituality in depth and include original textbooks extracted from David's three month online classes of the same name. Each module is unique but all include Audio CD's of workshops augmenting the class text. Other materials such as Incarnation card decks, the Incarnational Mandala, talismanic materials, audio/visual aids, and other items in support of the text and exercises are also provided in the packages. The modules are:

- **Home-Crafting: Self, Sacred and Blessing**
- **Space-Crafting: The Incarnational Self**
- **Crafting Inner Alliances: Working with Spiritual Forces**
- **World-Crafting: Manifestation and Service**

These Starshaman modules are complete in themselves as a comprehensive training. And, they can be used as the foundation for further development in World Service and other spiritual work. Each module includes two weeks online live with David Spangler. You may also engage these modules interactively with David Spangler online for two months as a systematic training.Additional fees apply. Please check the website for pricing, availability, and class schedules.

5. Sponsor a Lorian workshop or talk in your area. Please contact us for availability and arrangements.

6. Participate in Soul Friending. Our website lists several trained Spiritual Directors/Soul Friends associated with Lorian. They work with clients in person and by phone to deepen into their experience of the sacred, develop their spiritual practice, and work through personal spiritual blocks and opportunities.

7. Participate in Soul Friending. We can recommend several trained Spiritual Directors/Soul Friends associated with Lorian. They work with clients in person and by phone to deepen into their experience of the sacred, develop their spiritual practice, and work through personal spiritual blocks and opportunities.

8. Lorian also offers advanced training and longer-term programs for those who both wish them and qualify. Such programs can lead to certifications or a Masters Degree in Contemporary Spirituality (MCS).

9. Participate in the Lorian Associates. This world wide group makes up our growing community of people engaged with applying Incarnational Spirituality in their lives and sharing the results with each other. The only requirement for participation is to a working knowledge and practice of Incarnational Spirituality.

About the Publisher

Lorian Press is a private, for profit business which publishes works approved by the Lorian Association. Current titles from David Spangler and others can be found on the Lorian website www.lorian.org, at www.davidspangler.com, and at www.lorianpress.com.

The Lorian Association is a not-for-profit educational organization. Its work is to help people bring the joy, healing, and blessing of their personal spirituality into their everyday lives. This spirituality unfolds out of their unique lives and relationships to Spirit, by whatever name or in whatever form that Spirit is recognized.

For more information, go to www.lorian.org, email info@lorian.org, or write to:

The Lorian Association
P.O. Box 1368
Issaquah, WA 98027

Printed in the United States
120502LV00002BA/3/P